BLOG 2 BOOK

REPURPOSING CONTENT TO DISCOVER
THE BOOK YOU'VE ALREADY WRITTEN

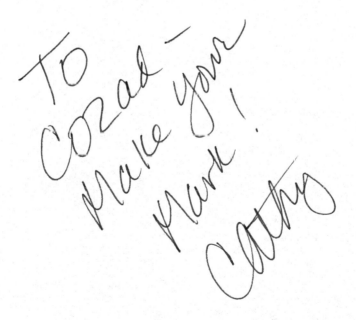

CATHY FYOCK

ADVANCE PRAISE

"I've learned from personal experience the power that blogging can bring to your professional career. I just wish I would have had a book like **Blog2Book: Repurposing Content to Discover the Book You've Already Written** when I started my blogging journey. Cathy not only gives you the reasons to start blogging but strategies for making the most of your content. A must-read for any writer."

— Sharlyn Lauby
author of the blog *HR Bartender* and
book *Manager Onboarding: 5 Steps for Setting New Leaders Up for Success*

- ➤

"We'd all agree it's easier and less daunting to think of writing a short blog than to even ponder writing a full book. Yet, brilliant, creative and book-savvy Cathy Fyock says 'Why not do both?" Cathy has created a roadmap that will literally get you from 'Blog 2 Book' in a clear, simple, systematic way in a short period of time. Picture your name on a book cover! If you've already been blogging, that vision can be reality if you get Cathy's new book and apply her wisdom."

— Elizabeth Jeffries
Executive Leadership Coach, Author

◄ -

"**Blog2Book** is a great resource for people like me who are starting their blog (in my case, on the topic of careers and calling). I am using ideas from this book to target the topics for my blog, testing content and concepts, with a goal of producing my own book in the near future. Highly recommended!"

— Mark Coile
Career Coach

"Writing your first or next book shouldn't be hard! If you blog, you have a book. Read Cathy Fyock's newest book, **Blog2Book**. She gives you all the guidance you need to turn your blog posts into a book in an easy-to-follow process. And she's even designed her book as a Blog2Book product so she models what it might look like for you. Highly recommended!"

— **Pegine Echevarria, MSW, CSP**
Motivational Speakers Hall of Fame inductee, Author

-->

"Repurpose, repurpose, repurpose! There's no need to start from scratch to write a book. If you're a thought leader who has already put pen to paper for blogs or articles, it's time to let Cathy help you repurpose that great content and get the credibility you deserve that comes with publishing a book."

— **Cara Silletto, MBA**
Founder & Chief Talent Retention Officer, Crescendo Strategies

<--

"**Blog2Book: Repurposing Content to Discover the Book You've Already Written** is a book that will be making a big difference to many solopreneurs. I've wanted a book for a long time but never got around to writing it. Cathy let me see that I've actually been writing it for the last few years via my blog! Now I'll have my book in record time!"

— **Lois Creamer**, *Book More Business*

-->

"Cathy provides a unique framework that simplifies the writing process so individuals can unlock their brain to write the book that already exists within them. As a professional who does consulting as a side line, I understand the importance of authoring a book to strengthen my credibility. Cathy gives practical information for busy people like me on how to get started by blogging. Cathy's knowledge and passionate enthusiasm are an inspiration to me as well as others who read **Blog2Book**."

— **Julie Scoskie**
Assistant Director, Louisville Free Public Library

"Cathy's **Blog2Book** was just what I needed to get my blog efforts organized. I'd played around with the idea for a couple of years, then started one but couldn't seem to get into the rhythm with consistent postings. Her Blog2Book coaching program and book changed all that. It's been a great experience learning to write consistently. Now I provide more timely and relevant information to my clients, and therefore give them better value and keep them more engaged. Thanks, Cathy."

— **Angela Greer, CTACC, RMT, CLYT, RYT**
Energy Health Coach, Speaker, and Author

"After having spent the last ten years writing a blog, while at the same time convinced that I could never write a book, I finally met Cathy! I had a sneaking suspicion that I could turn a fraction of my blog posts into a book, but how? **Blog2Book** is exactly the kind of how-to resource that I've been looking for. It's clear, it's easy to follow, and it's packed with practical ideas and suggestions to get you moving on your book. I'm finally publishing mine after ten years of dreaming about it. Thank you, Cathy!"

— **Lisa Braithwaite**
Public Speaking Coach and Trainer and author of *Presenting for Humans: Insights for Speakers on Ditching Perfection and Creating Connection*

"Cathy Fyock has done it again! **Blog2Book** demonstrates once again Cathy's ability to give the reader everything they need to execute. Her in-depth detailed approach shows you exactly what you need to do from beginning to end. Whether you are just starting a blog or have been blogging for years, this step by step approach to repurpose your intellectual property is brilliant!"

— **Jodi Walker**
Speaker, Author, Consultant

"As if by magic, once again, Cathy has found a way to address the common objections to writing a book by breaking it down and making it manageable. For those of us who rely on feedback and real-time inspiration, Cathy's plan to use existing or new blogs as a way to create our first or next book is a brilliant way to coax us into becoming the authors we already are! I'm excited to dig in and make *this* my new process for bringing my next written creation into the world. Thanks for removing another writer's block from the path!"

— Whitney Bishop
Change Agent for the Social Sector and
creator of the breakthrough framework Make 3 Changes™

"I'm a fan of Cathy Fyock and her books, and I particularly enjoyed **Blog2Book**. It is both practical and engaging, and I loved the way she modeled the concept in her book. Thanks for the inspiration, Cathy!"

— Whitney Martin
Consultant and author, *What's Next in Human Resources* and
Evolution of Human Resources

"For years I've told my nonfiction writing clients who want to write a book that they should start with a blog. A blog not only allows you to uncover your voice and test interest in your topic, it helps you establish credibility and build a devoted audience. Cathy Fyock's **Blog2Book: Repurposing Content to Discover the Book You've Already Written** is an excellent guide for anyone hoping to get into blogging with the intention of publishing a book. Her advice is helpful, logical, encouraging, and professional and will take you from wanna-be writer/blogger to published author!"

— Teresa R. Funke
author of the blog ***Bursts of Brilliance for a Creative Life*** and six works of fiction

Red Letter Publishing, Austin
Copyright © 2017 by Cathy Fyock.
All rights reserved.

Published by Red Letter Publishing, LLC
www.RedLetterPublishing.com

Book typeset by Kevin Williamson
Cover design by Kevin Williamson

Created in the United States of America

23 22 21 20 19 18 17   1 2 3 4 5

ISBN 978-0-9981714-8-7 (paperback)

B2B BOOK OUTLINE

This book is dedicated to all the writers who
don't like to write, but love having written.

LETTER TO MY READER

If there's anyone who knows how books can boost business, it's me. For nearly my entire career, my books have established my credibility as a thought leader, afforded me visibility with prospects and the media, acted as superb calling cards to get me in doors and close sales, and justified my increase in fees. More recently, in my years as a book coach, I've been helping my clients write books so that they can have this increasingly important business development tool for themselves.

Yet, as important as writing a book is, many professionals who know they need a book never write a book. Why? Because it's hard!

Even though I'm now a book coach, writing has never come easy for me. So, once I've written something and invested all that sweat equity into the project, I'm all for using that writing again and again. I'll repurpose an article into a blog post; I'll take a training program and make it into a workbook; I'll take a book chapter and parse it into blog posts. In other words, I'm a huge fan of repurposing your writing.

While meeting with a prospective client who wanted to write her book, she told me that it was her intention to start a weekly blog. I told her that if she developed an overarching theme for her blog, she could have the content she needed for a book in about a year.

"Isn't that cheating?" she asked.

"Of course not," I said. "If it's your writing, it's yours to use as you wish, unless you've already sold the rights to a publisher."

I've often told aspiring authors how *easy* it is to turn a blog into a book—and yet I've seen surprisingly few professionals make this transition.

1

This book is written as a road map for those of you who plan to launch a blog and aspire to become the author of a published book at some point. It's also for anyone who already has a blog and would like to repurpose its contents for your next (or first!) book.

I firmly believe that if you follow the steps outlined in this book, you can transform your blog posts into the book of your dreams.

You will likely find, just as I have, that you'll only need a slight change of approach for your blog posts.

For example, each post will need to be a complete thought, as though it were a short essay. Yet at the same time, each post will need to hang together with their companions through some common theme or thread.

You may find that you need to add some transition pieces. Some of your posts will be redundant and will need to be drastically edited or eliminated outright. Some may need to be part of your next book.

I'm "living the example" by crafting this book's chapters as 52 unique blog posts. Although most of these chapters have been written exclusively for this book, many are repurposed posts from my own blog and others are excerpted articles from my book *On Your Mark*. Finally, three chapters have been contributed by guest authors.

I've indicated the source of each chapter by including the following color-coded markers next to each chapter's title:

NEW POST

BLOG POST

⊙ **ON YOUR MARK**

GUEST POST

I wish you luck as you grow your business and start a lifelong habit of repurposing your intellectual property (IP) on the way to your own thought leadership!

PART 1
Why Blogs? Why Books?
Why Turn Blogs into Books?

Maybe you've been blogging for a while and you have developed a lot of great content that your readers value and appreciate. Maybe you've also been thinking about a book and believe that having a book could be important to getting the most value from the content you've already written (and worked so hard to write!).

This first section explores the benefits of blogging, of having a book, and the benefits of going from one writing genre to another. I'll share with you why short blog posts can be ideal for today's busy reader (TL;DR) when you craft your book correctly. I'll also discuss why I'm such a believer in the concept of repurposing your work.

WHY BLOGS?

Print periodicals are on the decline. According to Journalism.org, in 2015, weekday newspaper circulation fell 7% and Sunday circulation fell 4%, the greatest declines since 2010. Advertising revenue from newspapers experienced its greatest drop since 2009, falling nearly 8% in that same period. The newspaper workforce has lost about 20,000 jobs, or 39%, in the last 20 years. And three major newspaper companies—E.W. Scripps, Journal Communications, and Gannett—have recently merged, reflecting a trend toward consolidation in the industry.

People are not turning to print for their daily reading anymore. Readership of print newspapers may be declining, but rising in its place are online journals and blogs (from "web logs"). Blogs in general are growing in popularity and circulation—plus, there are always new ones to read, and there's plenty of business space to carve out one's own meaningful niche.

- ➤

Blogs are growing in popularity and circulation, and
there's plenty of business space to carve out
one's own meaningful niche. #Blog2Book

◄ -

Bloggers are writing about virtually every topic, in every industry, about everything from how to be a working mom to strategies for growing your business to tips for investment banking. They are written by marketing and communications professionals in large corporations, by small business owners and solopreneurs, and by individuals who love to write and communicate their views, sometimes just within their own close circles.

Just look at these statistics on blog growth and impact from written.com:

- Nearly 20 million people publish blogs on websites and social networks.
- 81% of companies consider their blogs "useful," "important," or "critical."
- 81% of U.S. online consumers trust information and advice from blogs.

It's no wonder that blog usage is exploding.

Blog posts may be of any length, but generally contain short, pithy posts of 350-800 words each. They are typically conversational; some writers make their own edgy, humorous, or thought-provoking.

Why do readers love blogs? As social creatures, we crave connection and community, and we feel connected to our tribe when we read a blog we care about. We are listening to someone who is like us, someone who can provide us with the insights and perspectives we need in our own lives and careers.

- →

As social creatures, we crave connection and community. #Blog2Book

← -

Blogs allow us to hear different perspectives and see the familiar in new ways. For example: as a Baby Boomer, I love reading posts from Millennials because it helps me see their concerns and issues, which are different from (and yet surprisingly similar to) my own.

Readers love blogs because they are accessible and easy to read. Let's be realistic: in our busy lives, who has time to read that thick, fancy business book we know we "should" read? Blogs are popular partly because they offer an alternative; it's much easier and convenient to digest short bites of information (as posted on a blog) than to wade through lots of details that you don't want or need.

Blogs are fun because they more often connect with current events and pop culture, which helps keep readers informed. Reading someone's blog, it feels like we're leaning over the backyard fence to catch up on the news with our neighbor.

Authors can begin blogging with no credentials, no platform, and no start-up capital. This makes it one of the most equal-opportunity forms of publishing ever available, and it means anyone can have a voice.

So let's get blogging!

➡ ACTIVITY ⬅

Do some surfing on the internet.
Find several blogs on your topic or industry. Follow these blogs.
What do you like about what the author does? What are they missing?

BENEFITS OF BLOGGING

Many speakers, consultants, coaches, and business professionals write a blog as a tool to communicate with their clients and prospects. If you don't have a blog already, there are some compelling reasons you might want to start one. Here's what you can do once you have your blog running:

You can repurpose the content you've already created. As a speaker, consultant, or coach, you have already developed intellectual property—your unique ideas, processes, strategies, and systems which make you more productive, efficient, or otherwise better in some way. Blogging is another way to share that content with readers who may become clients, and to solidify your professional/social circle.

You can establish yourself as a thought leader. With each article or blog post you write, you are adding permanently to your stock of knowledge as a thought leader. In time, you become associated with your body of work. You become known for your approach or your ideas. Ideally, you become the "go-to" person for that issue.

--➤

With each blog post you write, you are adding permanently to your stock of knowledge as a thought leader. #Blog2Book

◄--

7

You can share insights with clients and prospects. As you gain more experience and expertise, your blog offers a perfect venue for sharing new ideas with your current and prospective clients. It gives your clients ideas about what you are doing now and how you might help them with their issues or problems.

You can create your own brand identity. What do you want to be known for? In my first career, I was known (by choice) as a human resource professional with expertise in the aging and changing workplace. Now, as a book coach, I want to be known in a new space, and my books and blogs allow me to showcase my strengths and knowledge in this new area.

You can create content for your own book. You've likely picked up this book because you already have a blog and know its potential powers. You also know that the content you develop for your blog can be repurposed for your first or next book.

You can build trust and loyalty. As a blogger, you have a tribe of followers: friends, colleagues, clients, partners, and prospects, to name a few. By continually communicating with that tribe, you create a true following. These tribal members get to know you, trust you, and believe in you. Because you've built this trust and loyalty over a longer period, that tribe will be more open to offers for your products and services.

You can build a community with your tribe. As the blogger and "tribal leader," you are creating a community of like-minded individuals. You invite their comments and engagement; you can ask for their feedback on your thinking; you can even ask a question and ask others to give you their best answers. A well-maintained blog presence is better than two-way communication because it offers interactive communication with your tribe, especially as you incorporate elements such as a Facebook or LinkedIn group.

- ➔

As the blogger and "tribal leader," you are creating a community of like-minded individuals. #Blog2Book

◄ -

You can sell your products and services. As a consultant, speaker, or coach, you want to promote your services to clients and prospects, and your blog is a wonderful way to sell without being "salesy." Most small business professionals hate to sell *too* directly, but we do need to promote our businesses. By sharing client success stories, showing our approach, and demonstrating our expertise, we show current and prospective clients how we might solve similar problems for them.

➔ ACTIVITY ➔

What are the benefits you will derive from a blog?
Outline the benefits and circle the ones
that are most significant to you and your business.

WHAT MAKES A GREAT BLOG POST?

The rule about creating a good blog post is that there are . . . a *few* rules. (Not none, but not many.)

Still, while there are precious few *hard* rules for a great blog post, I've noticed that there are some soft rules—some common themes and characteristics.

They are well-written. They flow well. They are logically constructed. They are reviewed by someone other than the author, since we all tend to read what we intended to write and not what we actually wrote. They are free of obvious grammatical errors and typos.

They are interesting. What makes a blog post "interesting"? To put it simply, interesting blog posts offer their own new or creative twist on the subject. They provide a unique perspective or framing. For example, I'm working with speaker coach Lisa Braithwaite to create a Blog2Book, and her blog is about effective speaking techniques. Her posts include many unique analogies between speaking and other life observations involving everything from tattoo artists to sports figures to drag queens. Her perspective is different and quirky, and it causes you to think.

- ➔

To put it simply, interesting blog posts offer their own
new or creative twist on the subject. #Blog2Book

◀ -

They contain stories. Whether they're literal stories—or case studies, examples, illustrations, or vignettes—they illustrate the key point or message of the post. The stories can be fictional or you can base them on a recent client experience (with any names changed), but either way, they are there to show readers your key points in action and to breathe life into your words.

They are focused on the tribe. Who are your readers and what do they want? Are your messages helpful and valuable to the tribe members? Do they answer a common question? Do they address a need of the tribe? My friend Sharlyn Lauby, *The HR Bartender*, is always spot-on when speaking to HR professionals, and addresses her community's issues, from employee burnout to handling employee investigations.

They are accessible. Most blog posts are short; some as short as 200-300 words, some as long as 800 words (or even beyond 1000, in limited cases). Good blog posts are typically written in a conversational tone, with shorter sentences and paragraphs than full prose. Bulleted lists are common in blog posts for this reason; as busy readers, we want to quickly absorb the information available to us.

They have a consistent voice. Bloggers have followers because the followers can appreciate the voice of the blogger—and want to keep hearing it. Some voices are edgy, some are funny, some are nurturing, and a few are even controversial. But they consistently "are who they are," and their readers are likelier to stay.

They serve a purpose. Different blogs may have completely different purposes, even within the same overall topics. Some blogs are meant to educate. Some aim to give daily inspiration. Some try to give new insight or perspective. For many of the same reasons that they have a consistent voice, they have a consistent reason for being written.

Other qualities of good posts are not so prescriptive, or consistent. They may contain graphics or illustrations. They may offer a particular call to action. They may have catchy headlines or a grabber intro. All of these are helpful ideas, of course; it's just a question of what the author needs for his or her own blog post.

⊘ ACTIVITY ⊘

In the blogs that you regularly read, what are the characteristics that appeal most to you? Which will appeal to your reader?

IMAGINE—A BOOK!

Are you a brilliant professional who, like Rodney Dangerfield, can't get no respect?

Have you seen your career plateau, and without a route to continue climbing past your competition?

Are you frustrated that your big ideas are not being heard and given the consideration they deserve?

If these questions resonate with you, imagine for a moment that you have just authored your *book* . . . a real, finished, complete book that shows your expertise, shares examples of your accomplishments, and proves you're on the cutting edge of thought in the field.

Imagine that you have this book—your own finished book—in your hands. Imagine it prominently displayed on your local bookstore shelves. Better still, imagine it in the hands of that prospect you've been hoping to win, or being studied by your senior leadership team.

--->

> **Imagine that you have this book—your own finished book—in your hands. #Blog2Book**

<--

Imagine that, with your book, your phone starts ringing with job offers. Your computer is pinging with LinkedIn and Facebook requests and you have multiplied your online following.

Imagine your book as your calling card, positioning you as the one who "wrote the book" on your subject, effortlessly selling you as a credible expert.

Imagine being asked to keynote at a conference your peers attend, and imagine the accolades and recognition you'll be awarded for sharing your brilliance.

If writing a book is your dream, imagine that it could be your **reality.**

⊙ ACTIVITY ⊙

Dream about having your book.
Write a short story about your life as an author. Enjoy!

QUANTIFYING THE BENEFITS OF AUTHORSHIP

What does authorship mean for your business? Many nonfiction authors discuss the intangible benefits as having more credibility and visibility, having a larger footprint in the marketplace, or being seen as a thought leader.

But if you had to *quantify* the benefits of authorship, what would that dollar figure be for your business? I was discussing this question with some author friends who suggested that there are at least four ways that authors might quantify the benefits.

-->

But if you had to *quantify* the benefits of authorship, what would that dollar figure be for your business? #Blog2Book

<--

Increase in closes: You visit a client. That client is on the fence about you; maybe they're still considering another coach or consultant or speaker. The client is evaluating *you*, whether or not they should choose *you*. What is their deciding factor? Would having a book make you the better choice because of your perceived value, your visibility, your recognition in your field?

Ask yourself: If you closed 10% more sales, what is that dollar amount?

Added revenue streams: If you had a book, you could sell it at the back of the room when you were speaking. You could pre-sell the book before you presented your program. Visitors to your website could purchase your book. You could sell your book on Amazon. You could also develop other products based on your book and sell those. You could create an entire brand-new revenue stream just by selling your book (and associated products and services) in select places.

If you were able to receive 10% more in revenue from book sales, what is that dollar amount?

Increasing your fees: You are considering raising your fees. Can you "get away with it"? If you are an author, you have more credibility and visibility, and the client may be willing to pay more for your services because of your increased perceived value.

If you were able to charge 10% more for your services because you were seen as a thought leader, what is that dollar amount?

Increase in reach: Someone finds your book on Amazon, reads it, and is impressed. That person thinks, *I wonder if the author could come to our company and help us solve this problem.* Alternately: someone buys your book from you, lends it to a friend who has the problem you help solve, and suddenly you've just booked another engagement from a source you'd never even known about.

If you booked 10% more business because more prospects learned about your services through your book, what is that dollar amount?

Look at your revenue for the past year. Imagine that, using any of the above, you could increase your revenue by 10%. Wouldn't that be a strategy worth the investment of your time, energy, and money? And if you could realize a much larger return on that investment, would you even hesitate?

So let's write that book!

↪ ACTIVITY ↩

What are the benefits to you and your business for writing a book?
Run the numbers, and determine what having a book
(or a newer book) could do for your revenue growth.

6

🌟 **NEW POST**

TL;DR*

*Too long; didn't read

TL;DR is the Internet's shorthand for "whoa, too much." Wherever it's commonly used, commenters often leave it when someone's post or comment doesn't get to the point fast enough. Consider it the new-school version of Strunk and White's most famous advice ("omit needless words"), or of something Einstein once said: "Everything should be made as simple as possible, but no simpler."

Aspiring authors often ask how long their book should be. It's like when someone asked Abe Lincoln how long a man's legs should be—to which Lincoln responded, "Long enough to reach the ground." So how long should your book be? *As long as it needs to be to serve its purpose, and not longer.* Readers today want accessible, practical books, and often praise the "one-flight" books that can be read and digested on a single leg of a business trip.

-- ➔

So how long should your book be? *As long as it needs to be to serve its purpose, and not longer.* #Blog2Book

◀ -

When I'm asked this question about book length, I often think about a book I bought at the ATD conference where I was a presenter. I heard an excellent speaker, Dr. Andre Vermeulen, speak about the topic of his book, *Tick Tock This Makes Your Brain Rock*. I paid about $14 for his 50-page book; since it's loaded with photographs and illustrations, it probably only contains about 5000 words. Did I feel shortchanged? Not in the slightest! Dr. Vermeulen's book was the perfect summation of his (excellent) presentation, and it gave me precisely the information I was seeking when I bought it.

On the other end of the spectrum . . . I think about another book. When I arrived at another conference, I was given an advance copy of a new book from a well-known speaker. I was asked to sign on to her advance promotion team, and I excitedly did so. I lugged the thick tome home, and a few days later I received a call from her promotion team.

"What do you think of the new book?" the excited promotion team member asked me.

"To be honest, the book is still sitting here on my desk. I was really excited about receiving it, but it is so big and intimidating I can't even crack it open yet." The thought of lugging it on my next trip was no less daunting. I never did read that book. I probably never will.

The moral of this story: *less is more.* As a rule of thumb, 100 to 150 pages—or 35,000 to 52,500 words—is a typical length today, although there is no hard-and-fast rule. It's worth mentioning, though, that I've heard speakers talk about re-releasing books as two or three much-shorter volumes.

Some questions to ask yourself as you consider your book's length:

- Have I answered my readers' questions?
- Have I given my readers enough information for the book to be valuable to them?
- Have I adequately covered the most important elements of my topic?

Perhaps the most important question is this one: *Have I left my reader wanting more?* If not, pump the brakes!

➡ ACTIVITY ⬅

Pick up your favorite nonfiction books, and look at the page length. Are some of the shorter books your favorites?

ONCE IS NOT ENOUGH, OR THE ART OF REPURPOSING WRITING

I have never been a particularly gifted writer. It doesn't come easily or naturally to me. Never once did a teacher tell me, "You know, Cathy, you should think about a career in writing." Yet here I am, a book coach writing blogs and books professionally.

I've often said, "I don't like writing, but I do like what having a book does for my career." I've since heard that Dorothy Parker said, in a similar vein: "I hate writing. But I love having written."

---→

> I don't like writing, but I *do* like what having a book does for my career. #Blog2Book

←---

So, if I'm going to spend my creative energies writing and creating content, I want that content to count and count big! It should be no surprise, therefore, that I'm a huge fan of repurposing writing as a strategy.

If you think about it: as a professional or thought leader, you are constantly selling your intellectual property (IP). There's no reason that IP can't be repackaged for many different media, like speaking, writing, training, consulting, coaching, and so on.

Even when you're focused on the material itself, be aware that you can publish that written material in many forms and formats: blogs, articles, books, training materials, and whatever others make sense for you.

Let's say that you've just written a weekly post of 350 to 800 words. That's a short piece of content, but even so, there might be numerous purposes for that short bit of IP. The blog post could become part of your next book (as I'm doing here). It could be incorporated in a new training program. You could tailor it for a specific industry publication—or generalize it for multiple industries. You could write it for staff, then change it up for managers or senior leadership.

Similarly, but in reverse: a new exercise you develop for a client training program could be repackaged and used as a series of shorter blogs, or incorporated into your book. Or, if you've already published a book, you could extract chunks of that writing for short blog posts.

When moving from one genre to the next, you'll need to see what works and what doesn't. For example: when converting training materials into a book, you'll need to flesh out the stories or the narrative that wasn't written. When turning a short blog into a longer academic article, you'll likely add research and cited sources and beef up the content. If you move from a blog to a training session, you'll need to consider how to make the material interactive and engaging to make that material "sticky."

If you've put blood, sweat, and tears into your writing, as I have, then repurposing your writing is a great strategy to ensure you're squeezing the maximum benefit out of your own work.

➔ ACTIVITY ⦿

Have you been repurposing your writing? Consider the last article, blog post, or chapter you've written. What other formats could apply to this writing? Could it become an article, blog post, chapter, white paper, ebook, special report, workbook, handout, or something else altogether?

PART 2

Planning Your Blog2Book

Now that you're sold on the idea of turning your collection of blog posts into a book, let's explore some of the practical components of making that happen. For example, will all of your existing blog posts work for your book? How do you get started? What are the elements of planning your Blog2Book? Once you've written your book, can you go backwards and create other blog posts out of the chapters? We'll also discuss some of the basics—like making your plan, how to get going, and how to get in the flow.

IF IT DOESN'T FIT, YOU MUST OMIT

Suppose you've got a collection of blog posts that you are considering including in your book. How should you determine if those posts stay or go?

Is the post current and/or relevant? Is it evergreen? While your post was certainly current when it was published, does it still hold water today? If, for instance, your blog post featured Lance Armstrong or Bill Cosby as examples of strong character and leadership (as they once seemed to be), you might need new examples. While many posts will retain their relevance, some posts will become noticeably dated over time—especially if it involves technology or anything else that changes fast.

Does it reflect my own current thinking on this topic? While you may have felt strongly about an issue at some point, more recent events may have changed your perspective or adjusted your thoughts. When your Blog2Book is published, you want it to reflect your most current philosophies and ideas on the issues—or, so far as possible, the ways you have always thought and will continue to.

Does the book's thesis (and the blog posts supporting it) fit with my business strategy? I'm a strong believer that a business book should be closely aligned with your business strategy. In other words, the book you write should serve your business in some direct way: it should bring in customers, raise your position or credibility, and/or provide you with media attention. Your book can take you where you want to go, but only if the book and the thesis which defines it points in the same direction.

Does this post fit with the overarching theme/thesis? Every blog post you write may not fit with the overarching theme of your Blog2Book, especially if you didn't know you'd be writing a book when you started. You may, for example, have included a rant post where you attacked an idea more aggressively on one occasion; however appropriate for the blog, that post may not fit the voice and style of the other blog posts. Alternately, you may have written a seasonal blog post that just doesn't fit with the other posts. If it doesn't fit, you must omit.

--➤

If it doesn't fit, you must omit. #Blog2Book

◄--

Is this post redundant, or does it repeat what another post/chapter says? Throughout the year, your blog posts may issue a similar message in different ways. Blogs can be more repetitive; bloggers have to accommodate potential new readers, or people who didn't see every post, so it makes sense to repeat yourself on a blog more so than it would in a book. Ask yourself: does the reader of your book need to hear everything together in one sitting, or would that be too much of the same? Review your blog posts with attention to how they fit together when read all in one sitting.

Does the post fit within the sections of the book (if applicable)? If you have outlined different sections for your Blog2Book, does your post fit squarely into one of the sections you've created? Do you need to create additional sections? Can you combine sections together sensibly, in a way that allows the content to move together?

If you've decided that each post should read sensibly by itself, you'll likely have more work to ensure that the blog posts you've selected fit into the framework for your book.

Does it answer the questions and solve the problems for my target reader?
Perhaps the most important question of all: does the blog post I want to include fit the needs of my target readers, and does it offer them value? If the blog post doesn't serve a purpose for your reader, leave it out.

⊙ ACTIVITY ⊙

Review your blog posts and assess each one using the questions above.
How many posts will need to be eliminated, edited,
or modified to fit a Blog2Book book?

THE THESIS STATEMENT

A thesis statement appears near the beginning of a written work, and it offers a concise claim for argument—or a concise solution to the issue being addressed. A thesis statement is best as a single sentence; it can occur as more than one sentence, but it should be distillable to one sentence even if you choose to spread it out.

You should never confuse a *topic* for a *thesis statement*. The topic is what you're writing about; the thesis statement is exactly what you're arguing about that topic. The topic is the subject of our hypothetical debate; your thesis is what you actually argue in that debate. If a sample topic is "having dinner sometime," one thesis statement might be, "I think we should go to Harrod's on Sunday night." And so on.

Consider my book *UnRetirement*. The topic of the book was "the aging workforce," but the thesis was something closer to "employers fail to recognize the value that older employees can bring to the workplace." That's a single, concise argument, and it summarizes the direction of the whole book in one sentence. There's plenty of material to unpack, and plenty of answers that readers might want to hear from those claims, but the whole book is focused on providing exactly those.

The thesis is what gives you direction. Without a thesis, you're writing *about* something, as opposed to writing something. When my nephew Kevin was writing history papers in college, he was all too aware that plenty of people had written about, for example, the Civil War. But, to his immediate knowledge, his was the only paper which argued (specifically) that the Confederate "states' rights" argument was retroactive, part of Civil War memory, and not a motive for entering the war in 1861. Whether you like that argument or not, you must admit that *it is an argument,* and one with a clear direction; you can follow along, you can ask clear and relevant questions of it, and you will probably learn something from the paper.

-----------------------------------➤

The thesis is what gives you direction. #Blog2Book

◄- -

Good argumentative writing always has two important pieces. The first is a clear, pointed thesis statement, and the second is a well-organized outline. With those two things, you can stay on track with every word you write. In the end, style has very little to do with success, and grammatical correctness almost nothing to do with it (aside from meeting the minimum standard). Do your homework, and you'll be in good shape!

=====================================

↪ ACTIVITY ↩

Write your thesis statement. Print it. Post it. Continue to tweak it.

=====================================

"ASK ME ABOUT MY BOOK"
THE STORY OF THE MAGIC BUTTON

I often give aspiring authors a button when I meet them for the first time. When I give it to them, I explain that it's a magic button. Some laugh or smile nervously when I say that. "It really is a magic button," I tell them, "but only when you wear it."

The button says *Ask Me About My Book!*

---→

Ask Me About My Book! #Blog2Book

←- -

The button truly is magical—and I have many clients that will now testify to that magic.

The first bit of magic happens when the author gathers the chutzpah to actually put on the button—and wear it in public, where others can see it (and not under a sweater, as one client tried to sneak past me). By wearing the button openly, you set an intention.

"I *am* writing a book," you say by wearing the button. Even that's pretty hard for some aspiring authors, since they really haven't *owned* the fact that they are aspiring authors.

By wearing the button, you also create accountability with everyone who sees you wearing the button. It's likely that once you wear the button, someone will later ask, "How's the book coming along?" and you'll have to provide an answer.

But perhaps the button's best magic is its way of forcing you to fine-tune your thesis statement. When asked, "What is your book about?" you will have to state, time and time again, the whole compelling idea in just a sentence or two—in other words, your thesis statement. And you'll get feedback from everyone you tell, whether it's explicit in their words or implicit in their behavior and engagement.

Does the person lean in and ask more questions? Does the person suggest other stories or ideas? Or do the listeners suddenly need to excuse themselves? If the latter is the reaction you receive, it probably means you have some work to do in reframing your thesis, since it's not yet resonating with your readers.

If after 20 minutes or so you still can't tell the listener exactly what your book is about—or if you understand what you're saying but the listener seems not to— you have important work left to do. You should be able to tell people precisely what your book is about in 30 seconds, if not well under.

You'll feel the magic when your listener wants to hear more once your 30 seconds are up.

Do you need a magic button?

❯ ACTIVITY ❮

If you have a magic button, wear it to discover its magic powers.
You can also receive similar results if you place
"Author of the Forthcoming Book . . ." on your email signature.

WHY WRITE?

Getting straight on the purpose of your writing is one of the biggest hurdles to completing your book. If you don't know how you'll use your book in your business, you may fail to leverage the full value of your authorship—or miss the mark completely.

By getting clearer on how your book will benefit you and your business, you'll find that it's easier to justify and create the time you need to write it. You'll also find that identifying your purpose will fuel your motivation and drive.

---➤

> By getting clear on how your book will benefit your business, you'll find it's easier to justify and create the time you need to write it. #Blog2Book

◄---

Look at the list below and decide which of these possible benefits of writing a book best fuels your motivation for completing your book.

- To give to prospects as a "calling card"
- To help sell your professional services
- To establish your credibility
- To gain media exposure
- To develop a revenue stream from back-of-the-room sales
- To develop revenue from publishing
- To serve as the curriculum for your work with clients
- To launch your new business
- To demonstrate how you've helped others
- To establish thought leadership

- To open the door for speaking engagements
- To help audiences retain your message from your presentation
- To differentiate yourself from your competition
- To establish your value proposition with clients and prospects
- To showcase your achievements
- To educate your clients and prospects
- To create "buzz" for your topic and your business
- To challenge others in their way of thinking
- To say "I wrote the book on that!"
- To check it off your bucket list
- To provide it as a thank-you or giveaway to your clients, colleagues, friends, and family
- To leave a legacy
- To show a different side of the story
- To be cited by other thought leaders
- To grow your business
- To develop a fan base
- To be asked to serve on boards, committees, task forces, or other roles
- To get that nagging voice out of your head ("Why don't you write that book?")
- To tell your story and get the respect you deserve
- To gain visibility for internal promotions
- To snag the attention of business leadership
- To make a difference

Why are you writing this blog and book? By defining your purpose and creating a powerful intention, you'll be better able to achieve your goal.

➲ ACTIVITY ➲

Review the previous list and determine your top reasons for writing your book.
List them, and keep them in your current writing file
as fuel for your motivation.

AUTHOR AS TRIBAL LEADER

What if you thought about your "targeted reader" or "target client" as a member of your tribe? This is the framework that Seth Godin suggests in his excellent book *Tribes*.

What's the difference between a targeted reader and a tribal member?

TARGETED READER	TRIBAL MEMBER
ME VS. THEM	WE
HEAD	HEART
ONE-WAY	TWO-WAY
SILOED	CONNECTED
SPECTATOR	PARTICIPANT
CONSUMER	MEMBER

As an author, thought leader, and business professional, you want to create a *tribe* of connected, involved, and engaged members as a business development tool. Here are some of the strategies for engaging your readers so that they become tribal members:

Collect names and contact information for your tribal members so that you can connect with them regularly. Invite your readers to visit your website; use a landing page to collect this important data.

Create strategies for two-way communication with your tribe, including tools such as blog posts, newsletters, social media posts, and direct dialogue.

Communicate your genuine passion for your topic. Engaging the hearts of your members is as important as engaging their minds, if not more important.

Create opportunities to connect face-to-face with readers, which might include speaking at conferences, book signings and readings at book stores, and other direct engagements.

Survey your tribe to discover who they are, what they want, and what they like—in their own words—so that you can continue to meet their needs.

Connect tribal members with one another at conferences, through blogs and social media, and interactive webinars.

Identify groups or associations that share your tribal issues or values and collaborate to create useful, meaningful partnerships with these organizations.

● ACTIVITY ●

Review the list of ways to engage your tribe.
Which are you already doing?
What strategies might you develop?

FROM BLOG 2 BOOK

You have been writing a weekly blog post for at least one year—or have a stack of at least 52 blog posts. How do you go about turning this pile of posts into a book?

My friend and client MJ Kinman is an expert quilter who takes separate—and often disparate—fabric squares and turns them into exquisite art quilts (you can see some of her quilts if you visit her website at www.MJKinman.com). In principle, this is much the same as our work in creating a book from blog posts: taking disparate materials, which all have value for a single subject, and finding ways to stitch them together into an elegant whole.

It doesn't happen by accident. There is a form and structure to MJ's craft—and in the same way, there can be a structure to the way you "stitch" your blog posts together into a book.

- ➤

Create a structure to the way you "stitch" your
blog posts together into a book. #Blog2Book

◄ -

Step 1: Ensure that your blog posts each reflect what you want your book to be about and follow a single unifying theme. If you've been working as a HR consultant who turned into a book coach, as I have, it's unlikely that you'll be able to (or would want to) turn your blog into a single cohesive book. But if we assume that over the past one or two (or more) years your blog posts have reflected the theme of your intended book, then you can move forward. Scan the blog posts and see what themes emerge. If your blog posts have been consistent with your business theme, you should already know the general message of your book. (Don't worry if you don't have a title in mind yet.)

Step 2: Catalogue your blog posts. Review each of your blog posts; catalogue them on a spreadsheet with a name and number. You may want to add some contextual information if the title doesn't clearly indicate the message. If it helps, you might also add the number of words in each post. You should have at least 52 posts, but don't worry if you don't have them all right now—you can add to this list.

Step 3: Review blog posts and eliminate the ones that don't fit. Most likely, not all of the posts you've written will be right for your book. (Review Posts 6 and 7 in this book to eliminate the posts from your blog that aren't right for your book.) Some of your posts will be perfect, but others will be redundant, outdated, or ill-fitting. Some you just might not like. Some may not remain consistent with the voice you'd like to have in the book. When cutting, be ruthless but resourceful. Throw out what doesn't work, but keep ideas and idea fragments that might give you starting points for new posts.

Step 4: Check all of your posts again to see if any fill obvious gaps. If you don't already have material for empty spots, try to write the headings for any posts that would fill the spots. It's likely that your outline will have some holes. Review your existing blog posts and see if any will fit into the holes that you've created. If you need to write some new material, outline the headings. Don't write the entire blog post yet; you may decide after structuring the book that the titles or headings need to change.

Step 5: Break the posts into appropriate sections. It's also likely that there will be a natural division of the posts into sections along your thesis. What makes sense for your content? While writing this book, I've grouped the blog posts into process-oriented sections. Section 1 is about understanding your own reasons for converting a blog to a book; Section 2 is focused on planning that project; and so forth.

My fifth book, *The Truth About Hiring The Best,* is written *like* a Blog2Book—in that it contains 50+ short chapters, each about the length of a blog post. Each short chapter was a stand-alone thought, but since the book followed the recruiting and selection process, it was divided into sections that outlined the employment process (The Truth About Identifying the Best, The Truth About Recruiting the

Best, The Truth About Interviewing, The Truth About The Selection Process, The Truth about Selection Tools, and The Truth About Evaluating Candidates and Making the Offer).

If you choose to organize your posts seasonally within your book, the idea of 52 chapters is a good model. You could have four book parts each representing a season, for example.

Many authors will find that a thematic approach to grouping posts makes a lot of sense. If your book is on leadership, each of the sections might represent a different component or characteristic of leadership. For example, my colleague Lois Creamer helps speakers book more business, and she helps them achieve these nine key results: Increasing bookings, Developing a memorable positioning statement, Creating outstanding promotional materials, Identifying target markets, Qualifying prospects faster and easier, Answering sales objections and closing more sales, Finding the decision maker, Developing other revenue streams, Developing your "sales speak", and Gaining the competitive edge.

Step 6: Write missing blogs. It's clear now what you have and what you need to finish this book, so identify the headings for each "hole" so that you can write new material (or repurpose old material) for these sections.

Step 7: Provide connective tissue. What does your book need for the pieces to sensibly stick together? Perhaps it only needs a short Letter to the Reader to explain how to best use the book. You might want to add introductions for each of the book sections—whatever guides the audience smoothly to the end!

You'll also want to make your book a cohesive whole, so you may want to unify the language—make sure, for example, that you always use the same key words and phrases in the same way throughout (and with the same styling and spelling).

- ➤

Many authors will find that a thematic approach
to grouping posts makes a lot of sense. #Blog2Book

◀ -

Step 8: You now have a finished first draft! You'll still need to add missing pieces (Letter to the Reader, About the Author, Connect with the Author, etc.), and you'll have to spend some time reviewing the work on your own before it goes to an editor. I like to print the entire book out and read it in one sitting to see how it reads all at once. You might also want to send the book to your editorial board *before* sending the book to your editor. See more on editorial boards in Chapter 45, and ensure all the missing pieces are intact by referring to Chapter 46.

⊙ ACTIVITY ⊙

Create your "to-do" list for completing your Blog2Book book.
Create a project plan for completing your project.

FROM BOOK 2 BLOG

If you've written your Blog2Book book, you've borrowed heavily from your existing blog posts—but no doubt you've also created some new content in the book to fill its gaps. Remember: the same way old blog posts are "repurpose-ready" as book material, new material from your book is repurpose-ready for use on your blog. It's a two-way street!

If you end up using some longer pieces in the book, you may consider dividing each of them into several short new blog posts. For example, several years ago, I wrote a longer article of about 1500 words on "Writing Blogs, Articles, and Books to Boost Your Career," and divided it into five separate blog posts: "Developing The Topic," "Narrowing the Scope," "Developing Media Contacts," "Writing the Article," and "You're Published—Now What?"

If you've been published, there is no reason not to turn your book into shorter blog posts. When I wrote *On Your Mark*, we identified eight short sections, each of about 350 to 800 words, that could stand alone. We made a few minor changes, then added a byline that indicated that the article/post had been excerpted from *On Your Mark*. We also added ordering information.

- ➔

> If you've been published, there is no reason not to
> turn your book into shorter blog posts. #Blog2Book

◄- -

This mini-preview of the book was similar to offering a free sample chapter, which is a common strategy now used to promote books for online sales.

When excerpting a section of your book, a longer article, or a white paper for a blog post or shorter article, here are some suggestions:

Look for content that is complete unto itself. The content you select should be able to stand on its own without needing background information. It should offer a complete thought or idea, and not allude to other ideas that aren't contained within.

Make sure that the selected content has sizzle. Does the segment you've excerpted have a story or illustration? Does it contain a powerful metaphor or analogy? Be sure that what you've written has some punch.

Give yourself credit. When excerpting, let the reader know that this is from your book. You've whetted their appetites; be sure to let them know where to get the complete meal!

❯ ACTIVITY ❮

*For previously published authors, review your past books and
determine which chunks of content could be excerpted
for a blog, article, or other published work.*

🌟 **NEW POST**

DON'T FAIL TO PLAN

You might have heard the old adage: *If you fail to plan, you plan to fail.* Putting together a project plan for your Blog2Book is an important step in getting it done.

Too often, books don't get written because, while they seem important, they rarely seem urgent. In order to create a sense of urgency, you must create your own deadlines and milestones throughout the process so that you're moving forward.

--➤

If you fail to plan, you plan to fail. #Blog2Book

◄--

While there is no "right" timeline for finishing a Blog2Book book, it is possible to get it from blog to finished book if you follow the timeline I use with my clients on B2B projects.

Week 0: Schedule strategy session to discuss themes, thesis, working title
Weeks 2-4: Gather 52 posts; review; send to Cathy for review
Week 5: Submit final posts; approve cover; send to editorial board
Week 6: Send to editor
Week 7: Write transitional pieces, about the author, etc.
Week 8: Review edited draft
Week 9: Approve draft
Week 10: Format book
Week 11: Order books
Week 13: Receive books

I believe that the most time-consuming element of this project plan is in weeks 0-4, in other words, pulling together and reviewing the collection of blog posts you'll need for the book's content.

Be sure to block the project plan on your *calendar*, and not your to-do list. And as with anything else on your calendar: if you need to cancel an appointment, be sure to reschedule it.

⊗ ACTIVITY ⊖

Identify your 52+ blog posts and put them into one document.

DECIDE

Why is it that so many of us are frustrated trying to achieve our big goals? Author Steve McClatchy believes that our error is making decisions about these goals based on the faulty assumption that all goals and tasks should be managed the same way.

He explains that there are two forms of human motivation: Gain and preventing Pain. When we take out the trash or go to the doctor for our yearly exam, we are preventing Pain. But when we focus our energies on writing our books, going back to school, or learning to play an instrument, we are working for Gain.

Tasks that prevent Pain can fill your day and leave you feeling tired and depleted by the end. Gain tasks can make you feel accomplished and exhilarated. So why don't we focus on Gain tasks?

--→

**What in your life is worth defending on your
calendar for the upcoming year? #Blog2Book**

←--

McClatchy, in his excellent book *Decide*, argues that the only way we can experience true joy and satisfaction in life is when we focus on Gain since it is there that we are happiest with where we are and where we're going in life. Choosing to invest in oneself by going to school or writing that book—while putting more on your plate—will, paradoxically, allow you to experience a better balance and, therefore, more joy.

McClatchy notes that most of us don't get to our Gain tasks because we prioritize by urgency and not by results; for many of the same reasons, we are focused on our to-do lists and not our calendars. Instead of prioritizing by urgency (that the most urgent task gets done first), keep a list of *only* those key tasks that will give you the results you want (for example, "begin outlining my book"). Those are your A tasks. B tasks include important maintenance, and Cs are purely maintenance. By triaging this way, you focus first on allocating time and resources to those items that will get you where you want to go.

Next, he advises that you use your calendar to block out time for A priorities. If you want to write your book in 2018, you need to block time on your 2018 calendar. "The reason so many people fail to achieve their goals is because they have not committed to defending a time in which they will work on their goals," McClatchy writes.

So what is worth defending on your calendar in the upcoming year? Is writing your Blog2Book?

⊛ ACTIVITY ⊛

Read Decide.

NEWTON'S LAW OF MOTION AND WRITING

Newton's First Law of Motion states that an object at rest stays at rest and an object in motion stays in motion, unless something applies force to them. It's just as applicable to writing as it is to physics.

In the first place, it requires great *force*—willpower, motivation, time and energy—to begin writing when you are not writing already. In the second place, other forces will be acting upon you and slowing you down once you start; family, career, responsibilities, and basic needs will do the same thing to you that friction and gravity do to a moving car. But in the third place (and here's the good news), it feels easier and easier to finish parts of a project if you've been finishing them at a certain consistent rate.

You have to burn a fair amount of gasoline to get a car from 0 up to 70mph; it takes a great deal of force to "push" something that heavy from zero momentum to full momentum. And sure, you'll need to keep giving the engine gas to stay at that speed—plus, of course, you have to brake and steer properly. But if you're able to do your accelerating all at once, and then do 70mph the rest of the way there, you'll get there in less time, and with the least fuel burned. It might require your constant attention, but driving forward ultimately feels less like hard work and more like a habit of awareness. Again, it's the same with writing.

But let's forget cars and highways for a moment; you don't have to go at the speed of a souped-up Corvette, so let's not imply that. Think back to the old fable of the tortoise and the hare. Not only should you *not* think like hare— who in his arrogance puts off starting to race—but you (and all of us) should learn something from the tortoise. It took him all day to reach the finish line, sure, but he had momentum. He kept going at a consistent rate, and he got where he wanted to go, didn't he?

When I tell you to *write, write, write*, I do not mean to hurry you. I mean that you should be consistent in your work habits and persistent in your spirit. I mean that it doesn't matter what you write, but it matters *that* you write. I mean that, through the long night of drafting, you dance with every worthy thought, like so many masked suitors at a black-and-white ball. As Anne Lamott put it in her fabulous book *Bird By Bird: Some Instructions on Writing and Life*, "Don't look at your feet to see if you are doing it right. Just dance."

-->

It doesn't matter what you write;
it matters that you write. #Blog2Book

<--

Here are some ideas for creating momentum in your writing.

Start with the easy stuff first. Don't start with Chapter One. Don't start with the first sentence of your blog. Just start—even if it's in the middle, or you-don't-know-where. If you have a vision for some part of your book or blog, start there. When writing a book, the hardest chapters to write are, almost invariably, the first and last chapters. Why is this? Because the first chapter sets the stage for the entire book and the last chapter summarizes all that you've said before issuing a call to action. Until you've developed all the pieces in the middle, you won't have a clear idea about "the basics" of your book, much less how to summarize and wrap the book up. So go ahead—start in the middle!

Similarly, when writing blog posts, don't fret over your powerful and attention-grabbing beginning sentence. Just start. The beginning matters, but you can jazz it up later. You may even draft the perfect opening line while working on the second paragraph.

Dance in and out of your outline. If you've created a solid outline for your book/blog, then you can pick the part of your outline that you see most clearly and begin there. When you run out of steam working on a section, jump to a different part of the outline that you can also see clearly. See, you're making progress. And that progress gives you a "hit" of the natural feel-good brain chemical dopamine, which rewards you and rallies you to write something more.

Watch for road blocks that slow you down. Can't find the right word? Draw a line or mark that in red and move on. Can't recall that great statistic you read that you want to include in this chapter? Mark a spot to come back, then move on. When you're writing, write. Save research and editing for another time. They are distractions from your writing and they get in the way of your momentum.

Keep going even when you think it's crap. I can clearly recall times when I've been writing and The Bitch (the negative voice we all know) kept saying to me, *This is crap! This is crap!* Thank goodness I ignored that voice and kept on writing. When I came back to my writing, it was NOT crap. Yes, it needed to be edited—but then, everything I write needs to be edited.

Keep a word count tally. There is something enormously gratifying about seeing the word count add up for your blog or book. Each day you write, tally the total number of words you were able to add to your project. As you see the word count growing, you'll get a bit more dopamine and feel that much more inspired to continue the journey.

By focusing on creating momentum, you'll find that the journey isn't quite so arduous—and that you are, in fact, making swift progress toward your goal before long!

❯ ACTIVITY ❮

Pick one of the strategies listed above to help you
create momentum in your current writing project.

NEW POST

GO WITH THE FLOW

Don't you love it when the words are flowing effortlessly from your fingers to the keyboard? Isn't it bliss when you can see the book almost being created on its own? Doesn't every writer on the planet love this phenomenon we call "flow"?

Flow happens when you're in the writing groove. You're not even thinking. The words are writing themselves. Time slips away. You are *at one* with the writing. Yes, that's flow.

If you want to learn more about flow, check out some of the YouTube clips from the flow guru Csikszentmihalyi (don't even try to pronounce it!). He has studied this state of being and suggests that there are three conditions for flow: (1) structure, (2) ability, and (3) feedback. Let's explore how we can tap into these three conditions to ensure they are present when we write.

- →

> Flow happens when you're in the writing groove.
> The words are writing themselves.
> You are at one with the writing. #Blog2Book

← -

Structure. We can't "let go" until we know where the boundaries are. As writers, we need to have a sense of the parameters of our writing. For example, I've found that writers can do amazing things when speedwriting or using writing prompts or sprints. The rules for sprints are short and simple: no thinking, no editing, just writing. The writer is given a few words or a picture to relate to their topic, and then they go. I've found writers that can produce more than 100 words in a few short minutes when given this sort of structure—potentially over 1,000 words an hour if they could hold the pace.

Similarly, when working with authors, I've found that when they put a generic prompt like "work on book" on their calendars, they're less likely to achieve significant results. The highest productivity comes when authors can identify a specific task that they want to complete within a finite block of time. So, for example, I wanted to write this post on flow, and I gave myself one hour to complete it. While writing my draft, I'm about 20 minutes in, as of this moment. (As a note, I'd already done the research on Csikszentmihalyi and given a webinar on his three conditions for flow, so I was merely putting my thoughts from that program down on paper).

Ability. In order for writers to experience flow, we need to know that our ability matches the task at hand. One of the ways that we increase our ability, and our belief in our ability, is to practice. I'm a big believer in exercising your writing muscles, and in writing every day. Refer to Chapters 27 and 29 on daily habits and exercising your writing muscles.

Feedback. Do you have an accountability partner or coach to give you the feedback and encouragement you need? To be in the "flow," you need to know you're on the right track so you can let go of your worries and fear. By having a writing partner to provide you with that feedback, you can silence the critical voice (in *On Your Mark*, I call this voice The Bitch) and not worry that you'll embarrass yourself with your latest writing, or that you'll have to forever hang your head in shame. Having a partner to let you know when you're on track allows you to have the freedom to *just write*.

Are you ready to get in the flow? Ahh . . . what bliss when it happens!

---

❷ ACTIVITY ❸

What can you do to add structure, confidence in your ability,
and positive feedback to your writing routine?

PART 3

Writing Blog Posts

For those of you who are beginning a blog with an end goal of having a book, this section will be helpful. I'll discuss how to create great blog topics, how to write compelling titles and introductions, how to connect with your reader, and ideas for recruiting guest bloggers (so that you're not doing all the heavy lifting). I'll also share some ideas for brainstorming new ideas, and how to add muscle and beef up the posts you've already written.

BLOG POST TOPICS

Having trouble getting started with a list of blog posts? Here are some writing prompts that can be used to generate at blog post, or to provide you with ways to dissect and re-approach your topic. Anywhere I've included a specific number, you can change it to a number that suits you.

Your topic and . . .

- Step by step process
- Five mistakes
- Three problems
- Four funny stories
- Top ten characteristics
- Three pieces of advice (I'd wish I'd known)
- From the other side of the desk (or different perspective)
- Analogy/metaphor
- Historical issues
- Future focus
- Four surprises
- Little-known facts
- Perspective from a thought leader/client/partner
- Current event
- Case study – success
- Case study – failure
- Myths
- What NOT to do
- What TO DO
- ABCs

- Client questions
- Assessment
- Secrets
- Values/Beliefs
- Challenges
- Technology
- Global
- Diversity
- Most interesting facts
- More boring (but important) aspects
- Scariest issues
- Worst stories
- Best stories
- Your history with the topic
- How you became interested
- Your passion/love for this topic
- Your love/hate relationship
- Causes
- Remedies
- Implementation

◑ ACTIVITY ◐

Use the above list as prompts for writing sprints to keep your writing muscles exercised, and to provide you with content for your blog and your Blog2Book.

'TIS THE SEASON:
WRITING SEASONAL BLOGS

Seasonal blogs can have a role in your Blog2Book; after all, the target of 52 posts means one per week, and it could make sense to split up the book by "season" or theme. This is an especially good idea if want readers to use your book as a tool they will pick up and think about each week, or during specific seasons.

If you're looking at a seasonally focused book, consider these seasonal prompts:

- New Year's
- Celebrations
- Resolutions
- Reflection on the past year
- Visioning the future
- Winter/cold
- Snow days
- Groundhog Day
- Valentine's Day
- Relationships
- Love
- Presidents' Day
- St. Patrick's Day
- Luck
- Mardi Gras
- Spring
- Easter
- Graduations

- Memorial Day
- Mothers'/Fathers' Day
- Summer
- Summer break
- Independence Day
- Patriotism
- Vacations
- Weddings/Anniversaries
- Labor Day
- Back to School
- Fall
- Halloween
- Scary stories
- All Saints' Day
- Thanksgiving
- Christmas
- Holidays
- Gifts

Almost any special day can serve as a prompt for an upcoming blog post. Go to NationalDayCalendar.com to find unusual days you might want to celebrate or use as a fun or intriguing post; whether it's National Prosecco Day, National Garage Sale Day, or National Left-Handers Day, it could prove a stronger starting point than you expect for a blog post or book chapter.

⊙ ACTIVITY ⊙

Use the above list as prompts for writing sprints to keep your writing muscles exercised, and to provide you with content for your blog and your Blog2Book.

BRAINSTORMING TECHNIQUES FOR NEW BLOG POSTS

Need new content for your blog or book? Use these brainstorming techniques to help you generate new ideas and perspectives.

Lists. I love lists! And even better, readers love lists, too. They are easy to read and scan. Sit down with a pen and paper. Take a topic or aspect of your topic. I like using frequently asked questions (FAQs) as a common list idea to start. Give yourself a time limit. Make a list of the questions related to your topic. Then, go!

---→

Readers love lists. #Blog2Book

←---

Mind Map. Put your central idea or goal in the middle of the page. Then write other words or phrases that are associated with that idea or goal. Draw lines to connect and group key concepts. Many authors have outlined their books using this technique, and there are now excellent apps that can add new dimensions to this exercise.

Pros and Cons. Identify specific issues within your topic. What are the reasons for? What are the reasons against? This brainstorming exercise can provide the key content for a new blog or series of blogs.

Free association/stream of consciousness. Name a topic. Just start writing and don't stop. Keep writing for a specified period of time and see what emerges. The whole point of this tactic is that it starts out directionless—and that whatever occurs to you *without* direction might give you more insight or information to develop in your writing.

Client questions. What are the common or persistent questions your clients ask you about your topic? What are the odd or obscure questions that they ask? Providing answers to these questions can help create a blog post of high value to your clients.

Change POV. Say you've been solving a problem for Human Resources professionals who are interviewing candidates. Turn the tables and change the point of view. What are the issues that the job *candidates* experience during the hiring process? By changing the point of view, you add a new perspective to your discussion and help readers understand it from all sides.

Post-its. If you like lists, you'll like this similar technique. Instead of writing your ideas in a list form, jot each unique idea on a post-it while you draft. Then, group post-its around central themes. Look for interesting combinations of ideas. Consider how one item might generate an entire sub-group of ideas. Move the post-its around to create new linkages and ideas.

Impose a metaphor. Consider some universal symbols and icons: a lighthouse, bridge, tree, bird, eye, or anything else that strikes you. Now take your topic. Write as many comparisons as you can, however abstract or flimsy. (Or, first take the symbol, then write down words and phrases that are associated with that.) Next, put your topic next to that symbol, and see if you can come up with interesting linkages between the connecting words. Remember that, if this helps an idea work in your own head, it might be a powerful example or comparison for explaining your ideas.

- →

By changing the point of view, you add a new perspective to your discussion. #Blog2Book

← -

Hypothetical questions. Assume that your idea didn't work. Why didn't it work? Write a list of answers to that question. Use different questions to approach unique aspects of your topic.

⊙ ACTIVITY ⊙

Use a new brainstorming technique to gather ideas for your next blog post or chapter title.

TITILLATING TITLES

Great blog posts should grab your attention. And nothing is more effective that grabbing your attention that a compelling headline.

Readers might see your blog post headline five times, but they may only read the whole post once. This is why, even though it seems small, the headline is where you should spend a large chunk of your energy and creativity.

Unless you have a brilliant idea for the headline/title right away, don't sweat it. I suggest that you write the post first, *then* see if an obvious title emerges.

Great blog posts have titles that grab your attention. #Blog2Book

To discover the great headline lurking within your post, consider these ideas from Kevan Lee at https://blog.bufferapp.com/headline-formulas:

Surprise "This Is Not a Perfect Blog Post (But It Could've Been)"
Questions "Do You Know How to Create the Perfect Blog Post?"
Curiosity Gap "10 Perfect Blog Post Ingredients. Number 9 Is Impossible!"
Negatives "Never Write a Boring Blog Post Again"
How-To "How to Create a Perfect Blog Post"
Numbers "10 Tips for Creating a Perfect Blog Post"
Audience Referencing "To Anyone Wanting to Write the Perfect Blog Post"
Specificity "The 6-Part Process to Doubling Blog Traffic"

You may notice that many of these sample titles include numbers. It's not a must-do, but it's a good idea to use them where you can. For one thing, our brains like lists and numbers; they're tidy and discrete. For another thing, numbers are specific, and they help set reader expectations in advance so that it's easier to commit to reading your post (or chapter).

⊙ ACTIVITY ⊙

Review your past three blog posts. Did you use snappy headlines?
If not, rewrite them, using the suggestions here.

GRAB 'EM

Everyone wonders: what's the best way to start a blog post or chapter? Have you ever struggled with your opening sentence?

As you can see in this example, I like to ask a question. A question engages the reader, and if the reader is intrigued by the question, or has asked the same question, then you've hooked the reader.

How else might you open your post or chapter? I've outlined the techniques I've used in writing my blogs and book chapters.

Quote. Ken Blanchard says that 'feedback is the breakfast of champions.' You'll be stronger the more you eat it up. *I used this quote to begin my section on feedback.*

'To write is human, to edit is divine,' Stephen King once wrote. *I used this to begin my chapter on editing.*

Statistic. According to writer Joseph Epstein, "81 percent of Americans feel that they have a book in them — and should write it." That's approximately 200 million people who aspire to authorship. *I haven't used this statistic yet, but it's pretty cool.*

Story. "Let's face it. You're never going to feel like it," said Mel Robbins at the National Speakers Association convention in Washington, DC. "You just need to do it." *I used this story to begin a post on finding micro-minutes to achieve your goals.*

Let's consider a semi-fictional example. We'll call him Bob. *This is the beginning of chapter 3 of* On Your Mark.

Bold statement. Newton's First Law of Motion states that an object at rest stays at rest and an object in motion stays in motion, unless something applies force to them. It's just as applicable to writing as it is to physics. *I used this to begin a section of* On Your Mark.

Imagine . . . Imagine . . . are you a brilliant professional who, like Rodney Dangerfield, gets no respect? *This is an example from a blog post.*

Humor. A well-known strategy, but one in which I personally have no finesse. Many authors use humor to their advantage, and if you're comfortable using it, I encourage it. Just don't force the joke; I don't use this strategy because, in my case, it would too often be forced.

➔ ACTIVITY ➔

Use the above list as prompts for writing sprints to keep your writing muscles exercised, and to provide you with content for your blog and your Blog2Book.

  **NEW POST**

PLUGGING IN: CONNECTING
WITH YOUR READERS

How can writers build connection and engagement with their readers in a blog—and how does this differ when writing a book? Refer to Chapter 12 for more information on the role of author as tribal leader.

Titillating titles. If you want blog readers, you have to command their attention with compelling headlines. Similarly, throughout your book you should engage your reader with strong chapter titles and headings. See Chapter 22 for more information on writing headlines.

Attention-grabbing stories. Nothing grabs your reader like a good story. Use case studies, stories from your experience and observation, and hypotheticals to craft an absorbing tale that engages readers.

Ask a question and invite a response. And I don't mean just hypothetical questions, like many I've been asking. I mean that you might ask a question and request actual responses from your readers. If doing so, make sure it's clear to them how they can communicate their ideas, whether it's a response form on your blog post, a landing page on your website, or even just a link to email you. (In blog posts, or anywhere else online, you can embed a link that, with one click, starts a new email to you—just insert a hyperlink and use *mailto:youremailaddress@mail.com* like you'd use any other embedded link.)

Pick controversial and edgy topics. What are the most incendiary aspects of your topic? What are the gray areas where there is room for debate? How do different groups see the issues in their own ways? These are definitely ways to engage readers, but remember that sometimes edginess may be off-putting. Be sure that the voice of your message matches your values and the central premise for your topic.

Offer something of value. Do you have an IFO—an *irresistible free offer*—to give to your readers? It could be a special report, a white paper, an e-book, a list of resources, or a template—some tool that would be of value to your reader and that would prompt your readers to connect with you. It's usually best to collect something, like an email address, in exchange for the free value. Therefore, when you extend an IFO, be sure to use a landing page or opt-in page which collects the relevant data so that you can add these individuals to your data base and follow up regularly with information and product and service offerings.

Provide a forum for connection. Do you have a Facebook or LinkedIn group around your area of expertise or interest? This can be a wonderful venue not only for asking questions of your readers and encouraging them to engage with you, but it also offers an opportunity for them to engage with one another.

Let your reader know how to connect with you. Are your website, email, telephone, or social media handles included in your blog and your book? Don't make your reader look for it; if they have to look, they probably won't. In addition to a "connect with the author" section in your book with all your preferred methods of connection, provide readers with links throughout your blog and book inviting them to connect.

❯ ACTIVITY ❮

What can you do to better connect with your reader?
Pick one of the strategies suggested here for your next post.

YOU ARE INVITED: GUEST BLOGGERS

Are you tired of coming up with unique content for your blog every single week—or do you just need a little break? Why not invite a guest blogger to add their perspective? I've used a number of guest bloggers throughout my career, and I've served as a guest blogger for others when I've been able.

The benefits of being a guest blogger. You can repurpose your content or even entire blog posts or articles. You get additional exposure and maybe even pick up new clients or followers. You help out a friend or colleague who is just too tired or burned out to write the next post.

The benefits to you in having guest bloggers are numerous. You get someone else to do the heavy lifting for a change. You share a new perspective with your readers. You introduce a new voice. You provide your readers with a valuable resource.

- ➤

By having a guest blogger, you share
in the heavy lifting. #Blog2Book

◄ -

If it works in blogging, it can work in your book, too.

In this book I've added three guest posts, from writer Roger Grannis (see Chapter 38), from editor Barbara McNichol (see Chapter 38) and from writer/publisher (and my favorite co-author) Kevin Williamson (see Chapter 43). Each of these individuals adds a perspective that is unique to each of them and their background and experience. Hopefully, too, each person will also gain some benefits from helping me out here! Best yet: I invited them to contribute in large part because I believed that your reading would be enriched by their perspectives on their individual areas of expertise.

⊙ ACTIVITY ⊙

Who can you ask to be a guest blogger for your blog or blog book?
Consider your clients, colleagues, prospects, strategic partners,
fellow speakers and authors.

ADDING MUSCLE

Note: This also holds true when you are creating new blog posts. Where can you find new material?

Later on in the writing process, when you've got some sections finished, you might be concerned that there just isn't enough stuff there. It's a sensible feeling, really; you've been writing to no one in particular, and even though you do have enough knowledge and insight in your own head, not all of it will spill out. There might be enough veggies and meat in your fridge to make a goulash, but you may need to go out and find the right spices for it. (Or if you're trying to feed a big family, you may just need more of everything.)

As you go back, edit, add and clarify details, and cite sources, you'll use as much of your knowledge as you ever could. But in the meantime, one good way to plug holes, and to make progress generating content for the book, is to feed new meat to what already exists. In other words: you can build up rather than out.

Consider the following expansions:

Conduct an interview. Do you know an expert who could add some credibility to your book by sharing his or her insights on the questions you ask? Is there someone whose work you have used at any length or someone who created positive change in your professional life? Keep your ears to the ground for people who might be good sources; around the office, other people might be able to help you find such people, or might even be able to serve as sources themselves, though perhaps only informally.

Find something quote-worthy. Even if it's something people have heard before, it can be helpful to draw in someone else's quotable insight to help make your point. You do have to use quotes carefully, though. Using a good quote in your work is somewhat like placing a lamp in your living room; you want it to illuminate but not draw attention to itself, so it's usually best not to stick it right in the middle of everything. Quotes serve you best, I think, at the beginning and end of passages, so that they can either set the mood or seal the point. Putting a quote right in the middle of the point you're making is distracting and it steals your thunder; all of the credit you deserve for the rest of the thinking suddenly seems attributable to that person.

---➤

One good way to plug holes, and to make progress generating content for the book, is to feed new meat to what already exists. #Blog2Book

◄---

Mold yourself a metaphor, simile, or analogy. If you've got something written, but it's just not very "sticky"—that's to say, it's not very memorable, or it's a little dry—find a way to compare it to something else, however random the connection might seem at first. If you can use a metaphor to show how two things are similar, and if you use concrete, sensory imagery that engages the conscious mind, a reader will remember both things: your metaphor *and* the point it serves to make.

This requires you to play with thoughts, to ask yourself what the idea feels like, and to consider how you might explain yourself to a teenager, to someone who *could* understand but starts out knowing nothing about your work. In fact, this is a good rule for explanations in general: if you couldn't explain it to a child or to your grandmother, either you don't know what you're talking about or you need to work on your explanation.

Extended metaphors and similes are even better if you can manage them. If you imagine trying to explain the whole chapter (or even the whole book!) at once, and you're able to use a single extended metaphor or a set of related metaphors, please use them. When people read it, they will remember everything so much better. Besides, they will have enjoyed the book more as they read.

Dig up some numbers. Left-brained readers will appreciate appeals to data and statistical information, and even for people who gloss them over, the book seems more credible if you have that sort of support. If you have graphs or small tables, that's great (so long as they're compatible with your vision for how the book should look and read). This does create some extra work—aside from the research, you have to contextualize and explain all of your data, rather than just throwing it on top—but it will be worth it for you and for your readers.

Look through your older materials. Whether they are slideshow presentations, old articles, workbook pages, seminar exercises, or anything else, they might contain some insights that you had completely forgotten about. Leaf through all those resources and, on a sheet of paper, mark down all of the ideas you might want to revisit. Those ideas might cover different topics entirely—but good thoughts can come from strange places, and you never know when the piece you wrote ten years ago will be useful.

By adding muscle, and building up sometimes rather than out, you'll wind up with something more credible, more authoritative, and perhaps also more interesting. The process of adding muscle will also give you options for how to go forward with your project so that, even if you're not writing the next chapter, you're still creating valuable content for use sometime in the future.

➔ ACTIVITY ➔

*When you write your next blog or chapter (and it just isn't enough),
review this list of ideas to generate more meaningful content.
Or, use these strategies to come up with new blog post concepts.*

PART 4

Writing and Creativity

This section is for those of you who need to strengthen your writing muscles, find the time to write, and create daily writing habits. I'll also touch on important issues, like how to build your confidence as a writer, and how to avoid productive procrastination. I'll also explore ideas about accountability partners and coaches, co-authoring, ghostwriting, and writers' groups. I'll give you some ideas for getting unstuck and for finding your voice.

27

NEW POST

EXERCISE YOUR WRITING MUSCLES

If you wanted to run a marathon, would you ever just strap on a pair of tennis shoes and go out to run 26 miles without any prior training? Probably not. If I did that I would likely kill or injure myself, and long before the end I'd probably swear never to run again.

In much the same way, I hear about prospective authors who try to write their whole books all at once. It's no wonder that they become discouraged and disillusioned with the experience. They haven't been exercising their writing muscles!

It's important to begin training before we even think about writing an entire book. We need to consider how we get our writing muscles exercised so that we are able to go the full distance.

Blog posts are a perfect way to exercise our writing muscles. They are relatively short at 350 to 800 words, and they can help us hone our daily craft before we launch into the multi-week production of the 35,000-or-so words it takes to fill a 100-page book.

What are other ways to prepare for the marathon that is writing a book?

Exercise your writing muscles every day. Have you developed good daily writing habits? I believe you'll be better able to write the book if you've been writing regularly. See Chapter 29 for more information.

--→

Blog posts are a perfect way to exercise
our writing muscles. #Blog2Book

←--

Know your productivity. Just as runners who are in training know how far and how fast they've run, writers who are preparing to write books should know how fast they write. How many words can you write in an hour? And perhaps even more importantly, do you write best in the morning, or evening, or some other time of day? Where do you do your best writing—in the quiet cave or in the busy Starbucks? And do you do best with a large block of writing time, or can you chunk it out in bite-sized blocks of time?

Join a writing group or group coaching practice, or participate in writing workshops and retreats. When I work with my coaching clients, either individually or in a group setting, I always spend time leading writing exercises. It's not enough to talk about the writing experience; we need to practice. Similar to training for a marathon, we can be educated about the best strategies for keeping healthy, but it's another thing to actually do the jumping jacks, leg stretches, and deep knee bends. As writers, it is important that we not stop at reading about writing or talking about writing—we need to actually write!

➔ ACTIVITY ◉

Do a timed writing and determine your writing productivity.
How many words do you typically write in a one-hour sitting?
Do you know if your productivity is higher at a certain time
of day or in certain circumstances?
Do you know if you do best when writing for short, 20-minute
bursts or in one or two hour chunks?

28

COLLECTING LOOSE CHANGE

Do you know someone who has gone on a vacation or paid for some other big splurge purchase by saving their loose change? The same way you can collect pennies and dimes and eventually buy a beach vacation, you can find minutes here and there to eventually produce your book.

"Let's face it. You're never going to feel like it," said Mel Robbins at the National Speakers Association convention in Washington, DC. "You just need to do it."

Robbins is one of CNN's most popular on-air commentators and opinion-writers and is the author of *Stop Saying You're Fine*. She is known to millions for her TEDx Talk, "How to Stop Screwing Yourself Over." During her National Speakers Association keynote, she told us that we only have a five-second window to take action before the urge to do the right thing has passed. We often know exactly what we need to do, but many times we allow that moment to pass.

You may think you don't have time to write a book. You have a busy work life but you still want to spend precious moments with your growing family, or investing in your favorite hobbies and pasttimes. There are errands to run and tasks to finish. But how many times do you find yourself leafing through a magazine at a doctor's office, catching up on Facebook, or watching a mindless TV program—all time that doesn't help you (or make you feel better)—when you could be doing something, however small, towards completing your book?

We need to move quickly when we have an inspiration to act, which inspired me (at the time of this writing) to make a list of the actions we can choose in these little moments to move our books forward. The next time you have a "micro-moment," be prepared to take action.

Get clear on your thesis for your book. Once you know exactly what your book is about, you will have those issues on your mind as you go about your day. You may see great examples or hear powerful stories that add to your message. Keep a pad of paper in your car, at your desk, beside your bed, and near your couch—wherever you spent time—to collect ideas for your book. Or use your technology, like Evernote or the recorder on your smart phone.

---→

The same way you can collect pennies and dimes and eventually buy a beach vacation, you can find minutes here and there to eventually produce your book. #Blog2Book

←---

Take your materials with you. If you're going to the doctor's office or know you'll need to spend a few minutes waiting for your child after class, grab your folder of ideas and reread your notes. Jot down ideas that you'll want to expand upon, or sketch out your outline for the next chapter. My friend Angie spent some pool time with her daughter over one summer, and as she sat at the pool, she idly pulled out her phone and worked on her content outline. Reviewing her work later at the computer, she was amazed at how much she'd been able to accomplish in these bursts of seemingly-idle time.

Create very specific goals for each time block. It may be tempting to merely put "work on the book" on that slot on your calendar, but it's not helpful for identifying specifically what you need to do. (And that makes you more likely to skip or postpone the "appointment.") Having finite, discrete steps like "revise outline for chapter 4" or "rework interviews in chapter 2" or "flesh out opening for chapter 6" will prove far more helpful.

Track your progress. Keep a word count of what you produce each day. Angie, the same friend, started to keep a whiteboard on her refrigerator with her daily word count as a personal challenge. Mark, another friend and client, keeps his word count tally in a Dropbox file that we share. By tracking your progress, you'll be more mindful of how you are moving forward on your book.

Make a list of the gaps in your current manuscript. Make a list of the ten ideas you want to capture. Use lists to quickly outline ideas that can be turned into chunks of content.

Phone a friend, especially a friend who will push you to take action. Ideally, call an author friend who understands the *need* to take action.

Go to the bookstore or go online and conduct a competitive analysis. What did the competitors miss? What did they get right? How can you build on their success?

Interview a client or a resource. Schedule an interview and mark it on your calendar. Prepare questions in advance.

Call your coach or accountability partner. Get your colleagues involved in providing you with the support you need.

Write. Even if you only have five, ten, or fifteen minutes, write. You'll be exercising your writing muscle, and you'll be creating content you can use for your book.

Just like seeing the pennies, nickels, and dimes inch their way up in your loose change jar, you'll start to see your word count increase as you move toward completing your book—and the further you get, the more it will motivate you.

Remember that every small step moves you closer to your goal. Use the next micro-moment to take a small step forward.

➲ ACTIVITY ➲

The next time you find yourself waiting at the doctor's office or for your next appointment, pull out your favorite writing device (I like composition books) and outline your next post, or flesh out the outline for the new chapter, or reflect on the things for which you are grateful.

BLOG POST

DAILY (WRITING) HABITS

My mother always told me to drink plenty of water each day. I keep a carafe by my desk; I keep water bottles in my car. I know if I get thirsty that I've gone too long and am becoming dehydrated. When I drink my water, I feel more awake and less hungry, and I have more energy. It's a great daily habit.

Good daily habits are the ones that keep us healthy, on track, and in alignment with our goals.

Writers need to develop good daily habits, too. For them, that translates into some practice of daily writing.

Some days, I write articles or blog posts. Some days, I write in my journal. Sometimes I work on a new book project. But one way or another, I write every day.

It keeps the creative juices flowing, and it keeps that connection between my heart, mind, fingers, and keyboard.

What are you doing today—and every day—to exercise that connection? At the National Speakers Association convention, these were the best practices shared by those in attendance:

- Keep a gratitude journal. Making a record of the things for which you are grateful is good for positive thinking, but it also keeps the writing muscles exercised.
- Spend time each morning (perhaps while drinking your coffee), or before bed, to muse upon your topic and see what comes to you.
- Discover your "happy time" and "happy place" for writing. Maybe you're an early morning writer, or conversely, find that you do your best work in the wee hours of the night. You may be a busy

Starbucks writer, or you may need the solace of your cave to do your best work. Regardless, find the writing time and place that works best, and schedule time there.

- Identify your best method for writing. Some authors speak their books using DragonSpeak; some write long-hand in a composition notebook; others do their best writing by putting fingers to the keyboard. There is no silver bullet, nothing recommended by all the pros. Find what is best for you, however strange or specific.
- Schedule a regular call each morning (or each week) with a writing partner, accountability partner, or coach to outline celebrations and detail your writing intentions for the upcoming day (or week).
- Jot key words on cocktail napkins to capture momentary inspirations— or record ideas in a note on your cell phone. The main idea is to not only look for inspiration but to capture the insights when they strike.

--→

The main idea is to not only look for inspiration but to capture the insights when they strike. #Blog2Book

←--

- Block out time, anything from 15 minutes to two or three hours for writing. Block the time on your calendar and *don't* put it on your to-do list.
- Get your "head" ready to write by priming yourself. One writer told me he used noise-cancelling headphones, while another said that she turns on white noise (babbling brook or waves on the seashore, that kind of thing) to let her mind know *It's time to write*. One author friend puts on a specific "get ready to write" song as a cue for writing.
- Look for natural blocks of time to write regularly. One author described her one-hour commute as her "writing time" (the author "spoke" the chapter into a recorder while cruising on the highway).

It doesn't matter exactly what you do each day, but it is important that you create a daily practice that works for you. What's most important is that you write—and write every day.

Practice really does make perfect.

◉ ACTIVITY ◉

Identify your best daily writing habits. What works best?
What new factor might you incorporate into your personal writing time?

HEALTHY (WRITING) HABITS

Rest. Get enough sleep each night. There is a high correlation between hours of sleep and creative potential, so don't short-change your body when you're trying to do the big thinking on your book.

Nutrition. Be sure not to binge on comfort foods just because that's easier while you're working on the big book. Eat your fruits and veggies and make sure you're getting plenty of protein to maintain energy throughout the day.

Water. Remaining hydrated is a key to good health, and it's also a tricky way to ensure you don't stay glued to your seat the entire day. I keep a carafe of water next to my desk, so I drink at least 8 glasses of water most days.

Exercise. Desk yoga is a wonderful practice for writers. Stretching neck muscles, moving arms, extending legs and feet, and arching the back are not only stress-relieving, but can help writers get literal creative blood flowing.

Movement. Have you heard that sitting is the new smoking? Staying sedentary can wreak havoc on a writer's long-term health, wellness, and even creativity. I just got an adjustable-height desk that allows me to write sitting or standing—you can see what I mean at varidesk.com. I highly recommend it.

---

❷ ACTIVITY ❸

Stop and stretch. Stand up and walk around. Set a timer for one hour, and take a quick break. Grab a glass of water.

CLEARING THE DECKS

I recently spoke with Steve Bustin (at SteveBustin.com), a speaker colleague from Brighton in the United Kingdom. I learned from Facebook that he had written his book in one week, so I had to talk with him to learn his secrets.

While he used many of the same strategies that I outline in my book, *On Your Mark* (in fact, he had purchased a copy of my book beforehand), there was one central idea of his that stuck with me. He cleared the decks.

What does it mean to "clear the decks"? Outlined here are some of Steve's techniques, but I've also added some of my own that help you to get focused and get it done.

Work ahead. If you're going to write at the beginning of the next month, what will need to be done NOW to give you time to solely focus on your book? You likely have some commitments that must be attended to: client appointments, speaking engagements, revenue generating activities. What can you do now to prepare in advance? Do you need to pull together your meeting materials? Print handouts? Get out those invoices? Determine what is essential, and do it NOW.

Decide what can wait. Not everything on your plate is an A priority. What can be delayed a month? What can be eliminated entirely from your "to do" list? What can be delegated? Sometimes, when you prepare for a vacation, some items get put on hold; the same should be true for your writing project.

--→

Not everything on your plate is an A priority. #Blog2Book

←--

Turn off electronic notifications. Unplug your landline. Turn off your cell. Adjust your settings so that you don't receive notifications when you have new mail. It can all wait. Your top priority is writing. Steve adds: "To remove distractions completely, I removed the Mail app from my dock and used a desktop app called Rescue Time (rescuetime.com) which blocks your most-visited websites for a set period of time . . . it's stopped me sneaking off to waste time on Facebook!"

Notify friends and family. Put a "Do Not Disturb" sign on your door. Let friends and family know that you are totally busy. You don't have to say why; you only have to say that you are unavailable. You may need to define what constitutes an "emergency" with close friends and family.

Use noise-cancelling headphones or white noise. To totally clear the decks, block out unwelcome noises and sounds. I can't listen to music when I write (I'm a music lover, so I find it very distracting). Steve used noise-canceling headphones, then played white noise through them. You can get soundtracks of babbling brooks or gentle ocean waves—whatever puts you in that space ready to write. Steve recommends tinyurl.com/jpk9xhh.

Go away. Some of my clients and author friends find that the best way to "clear the decks" is to just escape for a few days, even a couple weeks. A writing vacation can be both fun and productive. I've often found that two hours of writing per day on vacation is like writing 8 hours at my desk in my home office. And on vacation, I have the added benefit of being rested and relaxed so that I do my best work for those couple of daily hours.

➔ ACTIVITY ➔

*Plan a retreat or schedule a few hours for which you will clear the decks.
What will you need to do to ensure you have
a time block without external distractions?*

32

🎇 NEW POST

I THINK I CAN! I THINK I CAN!
THE ROLE OF SELF-EFFICACY
IN WRITING YOUR BOOK

"I think I can! I think I can!" said The Little Engine That Could. The Little Engine believed that she could do it—that she had the smarts to figure it out and the persistence to keep at it. She had a quality that social cognitive theorists call *self-efficacy*, and it's the same trait that enables us to achieve our big goals—like writing our books.

Self-efficacy is an individual's belief in his or her capacity to execute behaviors necessary to produce specific performance attainments wrote Albert Bandura in his 1977, 1986, and 1997 research findings. It's the confidence we need in our abilities to be able to exert control over our motivations, behaviors, and social environments.

While speaking at the International Coach Federation Midwest Conference, I heard keynoter Caroline Adams Miller (best-selling author of *My Name is Caroline* and *Creating Your Best Life*) say, that self-efficacy is one of four traits that happy people possess. She also adds that research findings have shown that happy people not only achieve their goals, but are more successful; in fact, she states that empirical data show that successful people are happy people *first*.

- →

"I think I can! I think I can!" said
The Little Engine That Could. #Blog2Book

← -

So, what does it take to build self-efficacy? The good news is that we can control many of the components of self-efficacy. In other words: if you don't already have it, you can develop it.

Miller outlines four steps in building the confidence and tenacity instrumental for goal achievement. I'm adding specific steps you can use in building the self-efficacy you need to write your book.

1. **Have someone that believes in you.** It's easier to believe in yourself when others do. Do you have a spouse or partner to champion your cause? Better yet, do you have a support team? Napoleon Hill identified a "MasterMind group" as a team of peers who come together to brainstorm, share ideas, and affirm one another. An accountability partner can also be the cheerleader who helps celebrate your victories; a coach is someone who asks good questions and offers good challenges to help you discover your inner strength. In my role, I work both as an accountability partner and coach; I believe that when you follow my process, you can get it done!

2. **Have a proximal role model.** A proximal role model is one who is close by; it's someone with whom you have a personal relationship. I encourage my aspiring authors to hang out with other aspiring authors. You can learn from one another. You can share in successes and together figure out how to overcome obstacles. Group coaching programs, author meet-ups, and writing retreats are all great ways to build community with the people who can lead you to success.

3. **Develop good stress responses.** What are you doing to handle stress? I suggest strategies like practicing daily meditation, finding humor in situations, and getting enough sleep and proper nutrition. Daily journaling, especially writing in gratitude journals, is a technique for keeping daily writing habits and maintaining a positive outlook.

4. **Create mastery experiences.** Consider a "Swiss Cheese" approach to your book project and master small steps or chunks. Create calendar entries for daily writing. Practice writing sprints to keep your writing muscles exercised (I have recently added one or two writing sprints to each of my group coaching calls). Write articles and blog posts that can be repurposed later for your book. Practice "The Chunky Method of Time Management for Writers" as outlined in Allie Pleiter's excellent webinar and book of the same name (follow this link

to listen to the recording: https://attendee.gotowebinar.com/record
ing/1328200513792756481. For a complete listing of webinars, visit
cathyfyock.com/webinars). In other words: cut an elephant-sized meal
into bite-sized pieces.

If you follow these steps, you'll not only build your self-efficacy, but you'll also be creating the requirements necessary for flow. *Flow* is when your writing is effortless: time melts away and you're on autopilot, it seems. This is the writing state to which we aspire, when writing is actually fun. One condition of flow is that the task is equal to our belief in our ability—in other words, our self-efficacy. So following these steps will not only build confidence, but will lead to more moments of actually *enjoying* your writing.

As you're sitting at your writing desk, are you saying to yourself, as the little engine: "I think I can! I think I can!"? If not, it's time to step back and put a little self-efficacy in your diet!

❯ ACTIVITY ❮

Assess your confidence in your writing ability. Are you like the Little Engine That Could, or do you doubt your ability? If you lack confidence, examine one of the strategies outlined here and see if you can build your self-efficacy.

33

PRODUCTIVE PROCRASTINATION,
OR THE DOG ATE MY HOMEWORK

You've blocked your writing time, and now it's time to sit down and just DO IT. Only one problem. You now realize that you really can't write because . . . you should answer that important email. Then you realize that your desk is a mess, and you know you could write so much more effectively if you could just clear away all those distractions.

You've been there. You've met that demon. And its name is "Productive Procrastination."

As I work with coaching clients, I realize that there comes a point in every engagement when my coaching clients try to explain why they didn't do what they said they would do. And often, these reasons seem highly plausible, if not entirely rational.

My question, though, is this: is it a truly legitimate reason for not accomplishing your goal, or are you the victim of productive procrastination (which, by the way, sounds a whole lot like "the dog ate my homework" to my ears)?

I'm not judging. But I want to ask you the question: is this truly a legitimate issue, or are you merely trying to legitimize why you didn't honor your commitment to write?

Explore some of the following clever reasons why the writing assignment wasn't completed. You be your own judge as to whether you should give yourself a pass or own up to the fact that you decided to reprioritize your work.

- I needed to do some additional research.
- I decided on a different thesis statement for my book.

- I got a big client engagement and I needed to cancel my writing time.
- I realized I have too *much* information for this book.
- I realized that I have too *little* information for this book, so I'll need to do some additional research (see item #1 above).

--➤

Is this truly a legitimate issue, or are you merely trying to legitimize why you didn't honor your commitment to write? #Blog2Book

◄---

- The content outline (or table of contents) just didn't work.
- I needed to polish the story I'd already written (that doesn't count as writing time—that's editing!).
- I had to rearrange my office furniture so that I'd be more productive in the office.
- I needed to clear off my desk and clean my office.
- I started working on another important assignment.
- I don't know what happened.
- I had some important emails to answer.
- I needed to catch up on Facebook.

Every reason on this list could in fact be legitimate (except, in most cases, Facebook), so if you find yourself facing these issues, ask yourself these or similar questions:

- Is this truly a legitimate reason for not honoring my commitment to write?
- What would happen if I didn't do this item (right now)?
- Is this activity/task more important than having my book completed (or moved forward)?
- Can I make up the writing time I missed by cancelling some other task or activity?

- Will this task genuinely help me move my project forward, or is it merely a delay tactic for the real work I need to do?
- Do I believe I am worthy of having a book?

You be your own judge!

↪ ACTIVITY ↩

The next time you delay your writing because of a "good excuse," reread the list above. Is this truly something that needs your attention, or is it a case of productive procrastination?

34

BLOG POST

TEN WAYS TO SABOTAGE YOUR WRITING GOALS

You want to write your book. You want to get it done this year.

My guess is that even though you have every intention of writing your book, you may be unwittingly sabotaging your own best efforts. Explore this list of self-sabotages and determine if you are getting in your own way.

1. ***I haven't told anyone about my goal.*** If you haven't told your friends, family, and colleagues about your book idea, you haven't been using the power of intention to move you forward. By telling friends that you're working on your book, you will receive encouragement, and you'll become accountable when they ask you: "So, how is your book coming along?" My friend Angie was bold when, for this reason, she changed her email signature line to read, "Author of the Forthcoming book . . ." Some of my clients state their intention by wearing their magic button which reads, "Ask Me About My Book!" By wearing the button, anyone who wears one is communicating their intention to the world!

2. ***I plan to start soon.*** If you don't have a definite start date and time, you could procrastinate forever. It could be "starting soon" until the end of time. Put a stake in the ground. When will you begin? Mark it on your calendar.

3. ***It's on my to-do list.*** We generally work our "to-do" list based on the urgency of the task and not based on the task's importance, explains Steve McClatchy in *Decide*. Important goals, like writing your book, should be scheduled on your calendar and protected. If you break a date with yourself to write, you need to reschedule that time (and cut out the extra hour of mindless TV or video games).

Even though you have every intention of
writing your book, you may be unwittingly
sabotaging your own best efforts. #Blog2Book

4. ***I can do it on my own.*** We tend to meet our goals most consistently when we are accountable to a partner. An accountability partner can be a fellow author working on his or her own book, or it could be a coach who understands the process (and the pitfalls). Engage your support team to hold you accountable so that you can accomplish your daily, weekly, and monthly goals.

5. ***I don't need to have "skin in the game."*** We tend to have a sense of urgency when we are Preventing Pain (again, Steve McClatchy does a great job of outlining this in *Decide*), so it may "pay" for us to literally pay for something to help us towards our goals. Weight Watchers is one of the most successful weight loss programs in the world—in part because you pay to retain your membership. Many members think to themselves *I'm spending the money, so I'd better get serious.* Similarly, reaching big goals like writing your book might seem more doable once you put real skin in the game through a coaching program or similar investment. Thinking about benefits and costs, while important, is all theory—but it's action and commitment, not theory and abstract thinking, that will help you finish your book.

6. ***I have one more book to read before I'm ready.*** There will *always* be something more to learn. No one would ever publish a book if they wanted to include ALL the important information and up-to-the-minute updates. It's true: once you send your book to the publisher, it will be dated. But know that there are plenty of ways to make your book evergreen—for instance, linking your readers to your website for updates and latest trends. Don't forget, too, that you can always publish an updated edition—or another book entirely. Don't put off writing just because you don't have all the information; no one ever does!

7. ***I haven't put together a project plan (or I don't need one).*** You may think, I'll just get started, and write every day, and I'll get it done. But without a project plan, you may not meet your important goals—

actually finishing the book by year's end, for example. Without a road map that indicates where you'll need to be at any point in time, you may not get there on time—or you might miss the mark completely and fail to complete your goal.

8. *I need to tie up some loose ends (and complete some other projects) before I begin.* Other work will always be in the way of your book project if you let it. At some point, you'll need to determine which work is of the highest priority, and then devote time on your calendar (and again, on your *calendar* and not on your to-do list).

9. *I don't have a plan for how I'll use the book in my career or business.* If you don't have a clear plan for how your book will benefit your career and business, you won't feel the need to push on and complete your book. With any large goal, you should keep an eye on the real benefits of your goal (that you'll have more credibility, you'll be seen as a thought leader, you'll get more speaking engagements, you'll make more money next year, and so on).

10. *I want this book to appeal to everyone.* Go ahead and throw this idea away—completely. In the first place: if you want your book to appeal to everyone, it will likely appeal to no one. In the second place, it ignores the very definition of marketing: the practice of finding a *particular* group of people and selling effectively to that group. Think about it: people want things that are intended for *them*, that are specially written for people like them—because another word for "universally appealing" is *bland*. So target your ideal reader, and write to that person.

At a recent workshop I asked participants to write a letter to their ideal reader, which allowed the authors to hone in on the needs and concerns of their target market, giving them additional clarity on their book's thesis and focus. See Chapter 48 for more details.

⊙ ACTIVITY ⊙

How are you sabotaging your writing goals? If you are self-sabotaging, consider one strategy to undo that and move yourself forward.

ACCOUNTABILITY

An accountability partner is someone who will hold your feet to the fire and motivate you to actually do what you say you're going to do. As the name suggests, your partner is someone who will hold you *accountable*—who will require you to explain your progress or lack thereof, and who doesn't just listen while you share your ideas and aspirations (though they will hear those, too).

An accountability partner can be anyone in your life: a spouse, a business partner, a close friend, perhaps another author or aspiring author. Many people are well-motivated by a coach, whether the coach is someone who has served in that role before or someone who is fresh and new for the occasion. If you happen to know people with similar work, you can serve as mentors and motivators for one another. Their progress will compel you to make progress of your own; whatever failures or successes you encounter, they will be shared.

As a reminder, I am here to offer support, too. A large part of my business model is one-on-one coaching and group classes for people who are seeking exactly this sort of accountability and support.

Regardless, when you're selecting an accountability partner, you should consider the following guidelines.

- **Pick someone you respect and trust.** You should expect that your partner will have your best interests at heart, but that your partner also probably has a knowledge and perspective that you don't. You have to be able to accept constructive criticisms, to not take their edits and suggestions personally. Your partner(s) will push you, but they're never attacking you; in fact, they're helping you, and they won't let you down. If you don't want someone you know personally to assume this new role in your life, consider hiring a coach or a ghostwriter, someone independent who will serve as an accountability partner for the sake of your project.

- **Pick someone you see, or can meet with, on a regular basis.** Regular meetings require you to keep working so you have something to show at each new rendezvous. If you've done the work each time, regular meetings translate into regular feedback and support so that, after every meeting, you can leave feeling refreshed, reinvigorated, and motivated by the new direction. (Not to mention that just making regular progress of any kind feels good.) Many partners meet weekly; if your circumstances permit or even require it, you might meet twice weekly, especially if you're aiming to make a six-week deadline. (In my coaching practice, I meet weekly with six-week book clients, or twice weekly if writers want to be absolutely sure they'll have something in that time. I am also able to take ad-hoc calls between meetings.) The whole idea is consistent contact; if you don't allow yourself to get behind for a given week, you won't get behind over the course of the whole project—or what delays you have will be short.

-->

An accountability partner is someone who will hold
your feet to the fire and motivate you to do
what you say you're going to do. #Blog2Book

<--

- **Spell out your "rules of engagement."** What are your expectations and standards for the other person? What are theirs for you in return? Will you meet virtually or face-to-face? Will you take calls from the other person outside of your regular meetings, and if so, when is it too early or too late to call? Aside from creating an atmosphere of professionalism, these are good things to figure out as the terms that will work for a lasting commitment.
- **Share your vision for success.** Your partner should understand your goal and exactly why you're writing this book. This will give them a

certain amount of fuel so that, when your partner needs to keep you rolling forward, they know how push you in exactly the right way. It will also ensure that you have the same end goal in mind, which prevents the biggest sorts of misunderstandings.

- **Expect tough questions.** Your partner should challenge you when you miss deadlines. Your partner should help you understand what's holding you back. Your partner should poke holes in your logic, play Devil's Advocate, or ask the "dumb questions" that you wouldn't have considered on your own. Not only will this make the eventual book better, but it will ensure that the book actually gets written. If you encounter problems along the way, your partner will be conscious of those problems and will help you fix them.
- **Set specific benchmarks.** While deciding how meetings will work, you and your partner can decide what the standards are for the work you'll do between meetings. Whether you should write a thousand words, ten pages, or a chapter depends upon your timeline and your vision. If there are other tasks that need attention instead (for instance, conducting an interview or two), how should those fit into your weekly standards for progress?

If you choose an accountability partner wisely, they will be a source of encouragement, inspiration, and insight. They will also be there to celebrate your successes with you. They will, in essence, be an extension of you and your work. There are voices that we should ignore while we write, but there are others that we should listen to—and that is exactly what an accountability partner is there for.

⊖ ACTIVITY ⊖

*Who could you select as an accountability partner? Make a call
to your top candidate and have a discussion about whether
this relationship might make sense for you.*

CO-AUTHORING

For many of you, this will be your book: you expend all the effort, you reap all the benefits. But for some people in some cases, it might be a good idea to partner up and co-author your book with someone. Co-authoring can create its own challenges, but it can also lighten the load, and the final product might be better besides.

The benefits:

- **You're not in it alone.** Most people in the Western world are extroverts, and extroverts are "powered up" by social interaction, by other ideas, by conversation and collaboration. Writing is a largely solitary activity, which can make it doubly challenging for extroverts. Having another person share the project means having a constant source of stimulation, having a sounding board, and keeping a constant flow of ideas. Introverts can reap the benefits, too, since co-authorship is a flexible arrangement that still allows for personal space.
- **You share the work load.** Whether you decide to split up the content, or to have one person focus on writing and the other on editing, it means less work for both parties.

---->

Co-authoring can create its own challenges, but it can also lighten the load, and the final product might be better besides. #Blog2Book

<----

- **You bring different perspectives.** Even if one person is "project lead," as I was for *On Your Mark*, having (in my case) Kevin as a co-author, who then acted as a sounding board, helped distill the idea of the book to a purer form. A co-author will doubtless provide his or her own insights and fill any gaps in the other person's thinking.
- **You can lean on one another.** Co-authors have one another's backs— so if one person is struggling with The Bitch (our term for that negative voice) or just can't find the right words, the other person can spot them and help them through. If one person needs a little breather, they can afford to take it, knowing the other person will keep the project rolling forward.

The challenges:

- **You must create a unified voice.** No two people write the same way or from the same place. If co-authors "phoned in" all of their work, without finding a way to mesh it together, the resulting book might be schizophrenic and confusing. In order to prevent whip-lashing the reader, co-authors have to figure a good way to unify their parts. It's fine to have passages that are reminiscent of one person or the other, but like a zipper, it has to hold together tightly.
- **You have to divide the work load properly.** Whatever has to be done to complete the book, you have to agree on a division of labor, and you have to make sure all of your bases are covered by that division. Does it make sense for both authors to write, or for one to do the writing and the other the editing? Does one author do more of the lifting, or will the work be split equally?
- **You have to agree on a division of expenses, royalties, and spin-off work.** This is, of course, a question of fairness; if the levels of investment are different, the payout should probably reflect that. It's also a question of logistics: if co-authors are in different lines of work, in different places, or have different interests for ongoing work, it would be unwise to assume that both parties will be equally responsible for making things happen down the road. I'll give you some benefit of the doubt: if you're able to select a co-author well, making a good agreement should be very possible. Regardless, I advise that you put that agreement in writing for safekeeping.

- **You have to work out the logistics of development.** How, exactly, will you collaborate? Will you meet in person and look things over on the same screen? Will you email attachments back and forth and discuss them by phone? Or, perhaps, will you join the new wave and use a Cloud-based tool like Sharepoint or Google Docs? What level of oversight is needed with the work that is being passed back and forth? When working on *On Your Mark*, Kevin and I exchanged emails with attached work; I gave Kevin a blank check to edit as he pleased, though I reserved the right to rein him in and re-edit his work later. That was just the arrangement that worked for us; yours might be very different, and it's for you to figure out.
- **You have to support one another even if you're both in a funk.** It's one thing if one person struggles at one time—but what if you both find yourselves with your feet stuck in cement? If both people feel like giving up, they can help each other give up rather than continue working. Misery loves company, after all.

Some guiding questions for selecting a co-author:

- **Does the other person share your vision for the book?** If both people see the project's direction and end goals the same way, they can help each other get there. If, on the other hand, you have two very different pictures in your heads, you'll wind up going nowhere.
- **Does the other person share your passion?** Quite simply: do they have the heart for it? In our case—mine and Kevin's—we both have a passion for writing, and that lies at the heart of our partnership. Because of that, it tends not to matter that our passions manifest in different ways. In the case of *On Your Mark*, I am the businessperson, the pragmatist, the coach and consultant; my passion for writing comes from visions of growing businesses and making names for their proprietors. Kevin is the sounding board, the artisan, the wordsmith; his passion for writing manifests in bringing ideas to life and in honing the art and craft of the printed word. The difference has been complementary for us; we both love our projects, and even if we love them for different reasons, we're both invested, we're both passionate, and we can each serve the work.
- **Does the other person have complementary skills?** The other person won't have exactly the same strengths and talents that you do. However they're different, those differences should advance the project, rather

than leave gaps or steer everything astray. I can get ideas down on paper; Kevin can turn those ideas into colorful, fully-formed thoughts. I have decades of experience in my field; Kevin was a first-time author. Those differences allow us to cover a richer spectrum of possible readers.

- **Do you trust the other person?** Will your co-author follow through and meet deadlines? Will your co-author honor the arrangements about the splitting of work, and especially, the splitting of royalties and other fruit?
- **Are you interested in working with the other person in the long term?** There are no clean breaks here! However you might *imagine* this project as one-off, with a definite point of termination, you never know what will come of it later. Having both names on the cover is a permanent commitment to the other person—maybe not on the level of marriage, but it's totally different, either.
- **Do you like your co-author?** You will be spending a lot of time (and perhaps traveling) with the other person; even if you're not besties, you should be able to tolerate, and hopefully enjoy, his or her company. If you think the other person is a scumbag—even if you grant that he or she is talented—stay away.

This is all to suggest certain steps you should take when working with a co-author:

1. Decide in advance what each author's role will be in producing the eventual published book.
2. Come up with agreements that both parties consider fair, for both the division of work and the division of income and new opportunities.

- ➤

Create agreements that both parties consider fair,
for both the division of work and the
division of income and opportunity. #Blog2Book

◄ -

3. Develop your vision and voice for the book together. Include everything that both parties like; discard everything that is not agreed. Compromise; give the other person a chance to adjust what is being said so that it will please both of you.
4. Communicate early, often, and thoroughly. Stay on the same page. If you see the project changing course, whether for good or ill, talk with the other person about it and make sure you're both on track.

⊙ ACTIVITY ⊙

Have you been considering co-authoring? If so, schedule a meeting with your colleague and discuss the items listed above.

GHOSTWRITING

A ghostwriter is someone who writes your book for you and lets you claim the book as your own intellectual property. The most "visible" example of ghostwriting are the many celebrities and political leaders who don't have the time, drive, or skill to write a book by themselves, but who—probably for the same reasons that they have widespread attention—have enough good ideas and material to put together a book. Ghostwriters are also hired by lesser-known but equally smart experts who need something well-written to establish their credibility as thought leaders, or to start a new business, or to pull in new attention for speaking and other public engagements—but who, for one reason or another, decide they can't undertake the full book-writing effort.

Ghostwriters can provide a broad spectrum of services for their clients. Some ghostwriters do the lion's share, perhaps writing the entire book only from loose notes or certain primary sources; others act as uncredited developmental editors or co-authors for rough manuscripts that have already been written. Accordingly, the demands and price can run a pretty broad range—higher if they're experienced and doing more work, lower if they're inexperienced or doing less work.

These are the benefits of choosing a ghostwriter or contractor for your book:

- **It frees up your time for other work**. You contract them so that you don't have to worry yourself directly with the writing and editing, and so that you don't have to block out all of your free time. And, because this is their full-time job, the project will be finished more quickly than you could do it by yourself, under even your ideal circumstances. Hiring a ghostwriter can, overall, be a cost-effective alternative to putting your career on hold while you write.

- **Ghostwriters create intellectual property for you.** Again, the difference between a co-author and a ghostwriter is that, with a ghostwriter, only *your* name goes on the cover. It would defeat the entire point of a ghostwriter to give them credit. Clauses specifying that completed work becomes the intellectual property of the client are common in written agreements for ghostwriters; once that stipulation is made, you can independently do whatever you want with the finished work as its owner. Terms of compensation vary, of course, but their involvement stops when the book's writing is completed.

---→

A ghostwriter is someone who writes your book
for you and lets you claim the book as
your own intellectual property. #Blog2Book

←---

- **Ghostwriters can communicate your message better than you could.** Again, these are people who write for a living, who can make an opaque, cloudy idea as clear as blue summer skies. If you have the knowledge, but not the best sales or communication skills for that knowledge, it makes perfect sense to hire someone with those complementary skills. Someone who knows how to twist a turn of phrase, or who can craft a good story, can make all the difference for the widespread acclaim and popularity of your book.

The challenges:

- **It still takes time and effort to share the content and vision of the book.** Make no mistake, a ghostwriter can do a huge majority of your work for you, but that's hardly the same as saying that you won't have to work or think at all. A ghostwriter is a skilled hire, but they can't read your mind. However it works best for you and your contractor, you will still be responsible for educating them, for passing along or creating the materials they need, and for meeting regularly to ensure that what they produce is on track and consistent with your intentions.

- **The ghostwriter, for all his or her skill, may not have the style or sound you're looking for.** Ghostwriters are flexible, and can adjust according to your specifications—but they will have their own voice, and it may or may not be compatible with yours. If you find someone you like, consider a two-contract proposal. The first should be short-term and should function as a tryout; if you like their initial work and would want them to write the whole book, you would then sign them on for the rest. There's a certain amount of risk involved—you have to pay them for the first contract even if you scrap their work and try again elsewhere— but that's one way you just have to pay to play well. Even if you're out the first contract's sum, it's better to find out early than remain stuck with someone who doesn't fit—or trying to jerry-rig their work into something it's not once delivered.
- **Hiring a ghostwriter is invariably more expensive than doing it yourself—at least in absolute terms.** Not surprising, but it bears mentioning. Again, the decision to hire a ghostwriter can still be a cost-effective decision (since the time you're buying back is valuable), but ghostwriters are far from free at the time they're doing the work. The viability of this option will depend upon your available resources, your priorities, and your project. The viability of this option will also depend upon whom you hire and what exactly you'd like them to do.

One additional factor to weigh is the ghostwriter's knowledge of your topic. Sometimes you might want someone who's already versed in your topic, but other times, you might prefer a generalist who can offer a "cleaner" perspective and more layman-friendly language. Either way, it's certain that your ghostwriter won't know all that you do—just decide whether it's important that the ghostwriter has a head start and can write from a perspective that's already informed. Consider, again, that it might be an advantage for the ghostwriter to *not* specialize in your topic so that he or she can offer separate insights and keep the writing easy to understand.

When searching for a ghostwriter for your project, you should be looking at four things about each candidate:

- **Writing samples.** This will give you some sense of what range of work they've done, and more importantly, what sort of style they have. Be sure to read more than one sample, since they may show different qualities. If you like a ghostwriter, it might also be worth asking your ghostwriter for samples that are closest to your intended voice or subject; he or she may have more than what is first made available.
- **Knowledge of your topic.** Again, it's up to you whether you want a blank slate or someone with expertise in your field. If the former, gauge the ghostwriter's ability to engage your topic and draw connections in the writing; if the latter, look for someone closer to your neck of the woods.
- **Personality and professionalism.** Not only does their tone and style need to work for you, but it's important that you like your ghostwriter and be able to trust them. The ghostwriter is doing very sensitive work for you—and like selecting a co-author, you want someone who is available, responsive, and easy to work with.
- **Pricing.** Because writing is such a fluid line of work, no two ghostwriters will offer the same rate, nor the same way of structuring their price. "Industry standard" is slippery at best here. Still, you will need someone who can work within your budget and who can offer a good value for your work. Establish your budget (with specific reasoning and numbers) before you look, while considering a given candidate, do some math to see if they could fit within that budget. Some will adjust their pricing to fit a budget if it makes sense for them to do it; others are pretty firm. In any case, pricing will always make some difference in the viability of a candidate, and you should be conscious of that during the selection process.

⊘ ACTIVITY ⊘

If you can afford a ghostwriter, is it still the right choice for you? If you like this option, make a few calls to potential writers and explore how this relationship might work. I recommend a pilot project (a blog post or smaller project) to determine if this is a good fit for all parties.

💬 GUEST POST

SPEEDWRITING: CRANK OUT THE CONTENT
GUEST BLOG FROM ROGER GRANNIS

> *"Give someone a book and they'll read for a day. Teach someone to write a book and they'll spend a lifetime mired in paralyzing self-doubt."*
>
> — from Writerspace

It's true, isn't it? Writing can be a nightmare.

All kinds of things get in our way—mental barriers, comparing ourselves to others, fearing we have nothing to say that hasn't already been said. Not to mention plain old distractions.

Is there a magic formula to boosting productivity? A magic pill you swallow to make everything better?

Sure. Hire a ghostwriter.

But then the world would miss out on what is uniquely *you*—your experience, your perspective, your point of view.

And you would miss out on the act of discovery. British writer William Thackeray said, "There are a thousand thoughts lying within a man that he does not know till he takes up a pen to write."

It's best to accept the truth. Writing *is* hard. American novelist Nathaniel Hawthorne said, "Easy reading is damned hard writing."

While there is no short cut, no abracadabra, there are three ways I know to ease your anxiety and help you produce a regular, steady flow of vibrant prose.

1. Speed-Write

Start your day with speed-writing. Don't plan. Don't outline. Don't read what you wrote yesterday.

Pick a topic. Set the timer. And write. Fast.

Don't overthink, edit, or stop moving your fingers. Do not "write."

Jot down whatever comes to mind. Be wild. Free-associate. Brainstorm. Keep your fingers moving. Those gremlins in your head will run and hide when they see the words flowing.

How long to speed-write? Try three minutes. Seven minutes. Short bursts. Bing, bang, boom. This warms up your brain.

Once you've broken the blank-page barrier, try switching to the Pomodoro method: 25-minute sessions interspersed with five-minute breaks.

Soon, you'll have a first draft. Those precious first drafts, as rough and messy and disjointed as they may be, are the secret to success. You can't build a brick building without a big pile of bricks; you can't write a powerful piece of content without a rough draft.

Writer Anne Lamott said, "The only way I can get anything written at all is to write really, really, shitty first drafts." In a similar vein, Pulitzer Prize winner James Michener once said: "I'm not a very good writer, but I'm an excellent rewriter."

2. Capture Ideas

Once you have primed the pump with speedwriting, your subconscious will go to work—to be noticed occasionally delivering words, ideas, and phrases at random throughout the day (and night). Capture them. Carry a small notebook, recorder, smart phone, or index cards. Don't let these gems get away. Record them or they might be lost forever—don't expect to remember it again later.

A few years ago, I had to write a job-interview scene for a novel I was working on. I needed to come up with realistic dialogue. The next day, when I was sitting in Starbucks, a woman from the LL Bean store under construction next door took a seat at the table next to mine. Guess what she was doing? *Conducting job interviews!*

All I had to do was eavesdrop.

Ask and you shall receive.

3. Don't Call It "Writing"

The word "write" can shut down your brain. The thought of being a *writer* puts pressure on us, makes us feel like we have to come up with big words and long sentences—all of which results in writing that sounds clumsy, confusing, and stilted.

Instead: when you record your expertise via the written word, think of it as sharing ideas, providing guidance, answering inquiries, or giving instructions.

This mental shift will change your approach and free you up to *be you*. Focus on serving rather than trying to shine and look smart. You will sound much clearer and more authentic than all of the grandiose filler you came up with trying to be impressive.

Will these three tips cut your writing time in half? Probably not. But they can boost your productivity by 20-30% while reducing your anxiety, self-doubt, and zero-word days.

When Ringo Starr sang, "It don't come easy," he could easily have been referring to writing. Writing may never be a walk in the park, but with tricks like speedwriting, capturing ideas as they come, and calling the process something other than the dreaded W word, you will increase your page count, elevate your status as a thought leader, and get that exhilarating feeling that comes after finishing another blog, article, chapter, or perhaps even book.

One final thought. Simple advice from Nora Roberts, one of the most prolific writers of all time:

"Ass in chair."

It's that simple. And she's put away more than 200 novels.

So close Facebook, log out of your email, and turn off your phone. Sit down and write. Now. Today. Every day.

Do it.

Soon you'll be cranking out content at a rate you never dreamed possible.

➍ ACTIVITY ➎

Get out the timer and do some timed writing exercises. Pick a blog post topic, or perhaps a seasonal or current event issue that will tie to your theme, and write. Put 5 minutes on the clock. Go.

STANDING ON THE SHOULDERS OF GIANTS

One of the things I've told you to do is go to the bookstore or library, find the section where your book would fit, and scan through the titles already on the shelves. At first, this was an exercise designed to get your head in the game, to passively gather information, and to start considering how you'd like your book to feel. I'd encourage you to do it again, but this time, to examine books' contents in more detail and ask yourself a couple more specific questions.

What did they miss? What parts of a problem, situation, or institution did the existing books not pay enough attention to, or omit outright? Consider first how you might approach their book better than they did; then, think how you would write a completely different book (which you are) which covers what they don't.

What did they get wrong? Where do you disagree with what they say? Where are they lacking in evidence or perspective? If they're wrong in your view— are they universally, just-flat-out wrong, or are they right about pieces but seeing them from the wrong context, the wrong perspective, the wrong time? Even if not directly, is that error something you could call them on (even if not specifically by name)?

To paraphrase Emerson: it's easy to be humbled in libraries. #Blog2Book

What did they get right that you can use? Of course, this is when you might have to note the author, book title, and page numbers of what they "got right" so that you can pull out some good material and credit it later. "Good bits" might take the form of specific ideas, suggestions, evidence, arguments, or anything else that sheds light on the topic you're writing about. You may want to directly quote their work, and if you do so later, quote them in such a way that you can build upon what they're saying and add credibility in your own voice.

While you'll need to block out some time for this step, I don't expect you to read entire books as part of this; it's a good occasion to dust off your skimming skills from college. A good tip is to start with a book's table of contents; if something catches your eye, flip to the first page of that chapter and start looking for subheadings, topic sentences, and call-outs if they exist. Some books you'll be able to put back after thirty seconds; for others, you might need to limit yourself to 10 minutes where you learn enough to remember the book later. The idea here is to gauge the field, not to become an expert in the literature.

A final note on field research, and to paraphrase Emerson: it's easy to be humbled in libraries, to forget that the people whose books now fill those shelves were once young men and women in libraries. Don't feel *too* small while you browse; it won't be too long before your book is here, too.

⊖ ACTIVITY ⊕

Take a fieldtrip to the library or your favorite bookstore. Look at books in your field or on your topic. What did they miss? What did they get right? What do you need to expand upon?

CELEBRATE!

It's easy to finish something, put it down, and then jump straight to the next chapter, the next blank page—but that's such a disheartening way to work. It can make you feel almost like you did nothing of value, like you didn't actually accomplish any of what you just finished. Good leaders reward you; they pat you on the back for a job well-done; they make you feel like your work has value. Well, you're your own leader here; you should actually stop to give yourself praise and reward your own progress.

I suggest a few little ways to reward yourself. Do some of them, or hey, do all of them; you deserve it!

- Keep a to-do list of the next things you have to accomplish; it might be a to-do list for a chapter, it might be a really big to-do list for the whole book. Cross it off. It's done!
- "Turn in" your work somehow. If you have a coach, co-author, editor, or other cohort, send it to them. Even if you're by yourself, send it to yourself. Not only do you get to "share" that you've finished something, but you might get that relief that can only come from passing it off. It's out of your hands for a while. Breathe a good, hearty sigh and be happy.

Mood, morale, and energy all
feed into momentum. #Blog2Book

- Take a short break. Wherever you are, stand up, walk away, and do something else. If you want to cook yourself lunch, or watch an episode of the show you've been missing, go ahead and do it. You'll need to get back to work later, of course, but for now, enjoy your "nothing time" guilt-free.
- Treat yourself to something you enjoy. If you love Swiss chocolate, Naked smoothies, or going to the movies, now's a good time to go for it. Maybe you've been eyeing something in the seasonal catalog; as long as you can afford it, place the order. You'll get to look forward to it, and then, when it arrives, you can put it on and think, "I've been wanting this, and I get to have it because I've made good progress!"
- Celebrate with someone. Maybe save the champagne for when the whole draft is finished, but if you've been wanting to have a girls' (or guys') night out, or to go out for dinner with your spouse, this is as good a reason as any. Tell your someone, "Honey, I got this part done and I want to celebrate, so let's go." We're sure they'll be happy to have an excuse to celebrate with you.

Mood, morale, and energy all feed into momentum. You're doing more than just "keeping the monster fed" by writing; you're actually making steps towards something exciting and important for yourself. Let yourself be happy, and more than that, make deliberate efforts to reward what you finish. It will make the whole process seem fulfilling and less like a never-ending chore.

⊖ ACTIVITY ⊖

*What's your favorite way to celebrate? The next time you achieve a goal
or reach a milestone, be sure to take time to enjoy your success.*

NEW POST

WRITERS' GROUPS

Writing is a solitary business. It's easy to get stuck in your head and hear the critique of your internal critic (The Bitch). That's just one of the many reasons that writers' groups are healthy for authors.

Writers' groups can provide accountability, encouragement, and celebration. No one else "gets" us as much as fellow authors who struggle in similar ways to put one word in front of another.

You can find writers' groups virtually everywhere, since many groups are—you guessed it—virtual. In addition, there are MeetUp groups, community writers' groups (many of which focus on specific genres such as nonfiction, children's books, and mysteries), and writing workshops and retreats. Writers can also buddy up with partners who are in similar stages of the book writing journey by connecting with others in your network. You may find that groups like the National Speakers Association or the International Coaching Federation may provide a forum for like-minded authors who are writing to support their speaking and coaching businesses.

> No one else "gets" us as much as fellow
> authors who struggle in similar ways to
> put one word in front of another. #Blog2Book

You may also find writers' groups through working with a book coach. In addition to my one-on-one clients, I also have a group coaching cohort that meets weekly or every other week to share celebrations, hold one another accountable, discuss best practices and common obstacles, and learn new concepts. Each week my sessions, which are held via webinar, permit writers to have a forum to share and learn in community. They value the camaraderie and support from peers who understand the difficulties of writing. I'm also beginning a new Blog2Book coaching cohort, and I hope you'll reach out to me if you're interested in learning more.

Some writers' groups focus on offering critiques; some are merely for social support. Women Who Write, a women's writing group in Louisville, has its members share updates on current projects and do short readings/reviews for its members.

Be sure to select a group that meets your needs. Some groups are brutally candid and may offer very harsh criticism, the kind that an unseasoned writer may not be ready for. Also, if the group doesn't "get" you or represent your target reader, the group may prove more harmful than beneficial.

As an extrovert, I especially value a writing community. I need to voice my ideas among others so that they take full shape in my head, and a group of writers is able to give me that voice.

⦿ ACTIVITY ⦿

Find a MeetUp group in your community. Get your writer friends together for coffee. Participate in a writers' workshop or retreat. Look for a coach who offers group coaching.

GETTING UNSTUCK

There will be times in your writing where you'll be . . . a little stuck. Maybe your outline is perfectly fine, but there's a little catch in it somewhere and you just can't express the idea correctly. You're sitting there, mouth half-open, and you're staring at the screen, waiting for your fingers to move. And they're not moving.

This is *writer's block* and it happens to everyone.

There is no catch-all solution for writer's block; like the common cold, it comes and goes. Also like the common cold, it's annoying and you have to deal with it. Still, there are plenty of things you can do about it, and it's never too big a deal by the end.

-->

Writer's block happens to everyone. #Blog2Book

<--

The solution is *not* to beat yourself up or just "push harder" at what you're doing. Did you ever notice that when you're congested, blowing your nose harder makes you feel worse? When you get a cold, you have to stop, switch gears a bit, address the problem, and then go about your life a bit differently. Maybe you go buy your favorite cough drops, zinc swabs, and Vitamin C tablets; maybe you put on a heating pad and a pot of tea; maybe you whip out nasal spray or a Neti pot. Whatever you do, you do it because it helps you feel better and start to move past the cold. Likewise, there are some mental strategies to push through writer's block.

They all take some form of "playing with the page," of changing your approach from "just write" to "work out this problem." Look through these strategies, try a few if you get stuck, and figure out what your best remedies are.

Pretend it's a puzzle like any other puzzle. If you frequent Sudoku puzzles or crosswords, you know that "stuck" feeling. But, as you know, rarely do you sit there and beat your head against the desk for more than a couple minutes on a single part of one problem.

For Sudoku, people tend to examine the problem from one angle at a time—that is, by rows or columns or boxes. If you're stuck in Sudoku, it helps to switch gears and look somewhere else in the puzzle, or focus on boxes instead of columns. For crosswords, it's usually helpful to do one of two things: either you go somewhere else in the puzzle to try and generate more letters, or you rethink the clue you're stuck on. Maybe you should be thinking of a noun and not a verb for the answer. In all of these cases: you have to rethink your thinking. Maybe you shouldn't be trying to think about it *this* way, but you should be thinking about it some other way.

- ➤

You need to rethink your thinking. #Blog2Book

◄ -

Use stream-of-consciousness. Rethinking and evasion are complementary strategies. If something is getting in your way, you take two steps to the right. Not only do the lateral steps mean you can see around obstacles now, but it also means that you can just keep walking past it if you wish—so long as you wind up back on track.

"Stream of consciousness" just means that you write exactly what you're thinking, moment by moment. It's a highly spontaneous strategy, and as such, you have to be willing to accept that you'll be creating a lot of filler as you write. That's okay. Editing later will be easier. The idea here is that, as long as the idea is in there somewhere, you can just sling everything around and you'll then be able to find what you're looking for.

It's like the "dump strategy" everyone has used to find one small object in a clumsy bag of things. Ever been looking for Tic-Tacs in your purse, and you know they're in there somewhere, and after a minute of looking you just say *to hell with it* and dump the contents of your purse onto the table? There may (or may not) be a moment of embarrassment, and then you need a minute to put everything back—but you did find the damn Tic-Tacs, didn't you?

Conjure up your best friend, colleague, or confidante. This is the person to whom you can say anything, and he or she just listen. Explain to this person where you're stuck. Imagine this person sitting there, eyes on you, nodding along.

You say you're stuck.

"All right. What are you trying to say?"

Well, I'm here in the chapter and idea, and the next step is like this, but I don't know how to bridge the ideas, or how to put it right.

"Explain it to me."

OK. It's like this. After you've finished these steps in my plan, you have to—

"Stop. Whatever you're about to say to me, write it down."

And so you do.

It's the combination of friendliness (you're not intimidated or put off by this person) and directness (they ask you point-blank "what are you trying to say?") that can help coax out the idea. Sometimes, the antidote to writer's block is a little bit of company—a sounding board.

You can probably manage by imagining them there, but we won't discourage you from actually giving them a call if it helps you.

Stimulate your senses. Part of the problem might be the flatness of the situation: the hum of your computer screen, the nothingness of the walls, silence in the room. Pull out a few good CDs from your collection; try playing a few favorites. It doesn't have to be Mozart or Beethoven, any of the tunes they play to teach toddlers algebra. Try some good dance numbers or something from your high school or college days. If you've got some good "rainy day" music, pull that out too—and maybe add white noise like RainyMood.com in the background.

For the bloodhound in all of us, head over to the candle shop while you're out to go to the bookstore. Spend a while sniffing everything. If you love the smell of the ocean, or the woods, or clean linens, or freshly baked cookies, there's something in there for you. The idea is to find something that will make you grin every time you smell it, something that both calms and invigorates you. Buy one, light it in your office, and try working with that smell in the air.

Sometimes, you just need caffeine or a piece of candy. If being able to sip from your cup of octane helps, or if you get a little burst of good energy every time you've got dark chocolate on your tongue, make those things available to yourself.

Of course, don't overdo it here. We don't want you to drink too much coffee and then re-enact that scene from *Risky Business* while your house (which smells deliciously of blue agave and bamboo) begins to burn down around you. But if ever you imagined writers as grumpy anorexics who bang away on an old typewriter in a dark room, you can lay that worry to rest for yourself. (In fact, many a good author has been a little too hedonistic, shall we say.) Enjoy yourself while you write; no reason not to.

Doodle. If you're writing on the computer (which we assume many of you will), sometimes it's helpful to remember what your fingers can do with more freedom. That can mean something as simple as picking up a pen and jotting down your thoughts on whatever is causing writer's block. While you're doing that, feel free to zone out, like all of us did in trigonometry class, and just have a little fun with the pen. Draw this, make bubble letters out of that, and so on. If you doodle in a semi-conscious way, it can actually help you develop ideas and get around writer's block. If nothing else, it will give your mind a little break so that you don't feel so stumped when you focus again.

- ➤

Enjoy yourself while you write; no reason not to. #Blog2Book

◄ -

Google. In the twenty-first century, a little inspiration is only a click away. Use our favorite search engine to dig up quotes, inspiration, definitions and information, relevant ideas, and anything else that gets your mind turning. Don't get distracted—the rest of the Internet is, of course, an infinite well of nothingness—but by the same token, you can find nearly anything you might need on the Internet. That includes ways to solve writing problems and to keep yourself interested in the topic of your project.

❯ ACTIVITY ❮

The next time you're stuck, try a new technique. If you haven't tried Googling the topic, give it a shot. If you're not a doodler, try it. Inspiration can be found in looking at your problems differently.

43 💬 GUEST POST

FINDING YOUR VOICE
GUEST BLOG FROM KEVIN WILLIAMSON

Writers often discuss their "voice," or the process of "finding their voice"— and to the extent that *finding one's voice* is a real phenomenon, it's very important to good writing. But it's one aspect of writing that prospective authors overthink too often; on a bad day, a new author's sense that you've "lost your voice" is enough for anyone to put down the pen and not write at all. And what a loss that would be.

To make some substance of the matter, let's start with what most people *think* a writer's "voice" is—as shown by all the language we use around voice. Your writing voice is something you "find"; novice writers don't have a voice yet, or so the thinking goes. And here's a confusing thought we have about a writer's voice: that it somehow has nothing to do with our *actual* voice, the one we've been using for years without a second thought.

Maybe you see some of the problems already. Your writing voice can't be something you *find*—it's a part of yourself, not a tool you pick up and start using. And as it turns out, your writing voice is not all that different from the real voice you use every day—so let's stop thinking otherwise.

--→

Your writing voice can't be something you find—it's a part of yourself, not a tool you pick up and start using. #Blog2Book

←--

Let me instead offer a simple definition—not of "voice" itself, but what it looks like to find yours. **A writer who has found their voice has full confidence in what they have uniquely written and the way they have uniquely written it.**

117

That's it—easier said than done, but simple enough to assess.

Many of you are speakers, or could imagine people like yourself on stage. What's the difference between someone who "has their voice" on stage and someone who doesn't? The answer most people give would probably boil down to *confidence*—whether the speaker looks comfortable and honest saying what they do. The presentations that make the audience uncomfortable—or that just aren't memorable—are invariably the ones where the speaker falters, whether in preparation or some element of self-presentation.

Human beings are much better mind readers than they credit themselves for. Most of us already know when someone isn't comfortable; we just don't say so aloud. We can smell fear; we can tell when someone knows less (or more) than they say. Why should it be any different on the page? Don't you think there's a difference you can spot between confident writing and unconfident writing? (Does it seem like I doubt any of what I've written here?)

"Finding your voice" in your writing is no different from finding your voice on a stage, or finding your sense of humor, or finding the nerve to do anything dangerous or exciting. It's already a part of you; it's just a matter of definition and practice (and motivation). Can you find one sentence you've written that's "close to home," that *feels* like you, that seems to give you a little courage when you read it aloud? That little extra courage is confidence, and that's the feeling of being fully focused on an idea that's genuinely important to you. Consider that, if knowledge is what you use to build bridges from one idea to another, confidence is what lets you traverse bridges even when there are gaps; you need to be confident to lead others from one another to the next fluidly, and when gaps in knowledge are inevitable.

Even in your best work, there might only be several surges of that confidence, where your words seem to take on power for a moment that could fill cathedrals and stadiums—but the rest, even if lacking the same verve and scale, should have the same level of comfort and honesty. If you—or your book—can arrive at the presentation prepared and comfortable, knowing what you know and ready to say what you're there to say—and better yet, if you visibly know more than you need to and select the best details for the audience—it'll attract genuine interest, the kind that sells. Those key words and phrases you've tuned so much, and that always meant so much to you, will become the hooks on which the rest of your work hangs in the audience's mind. Those will give them the confidence to follow you wherever you take them.

When writers continue to say they "found their voice," it isn't dishonest, no matter how little it may resemble the truth. After all, each of us wakes up some mornings and realizes we're further than we were in the past, that we're comfortable or capable in ways we never imagined we'd be. With enough practice (especially daily practice), writers stop fidgeting about little worries and insecurities and begin drafting paragraphs in much the same way they'd speak them aloud, or with a similar effortlessness. Someday after that becomes habit, we might wake up and realize we don't struggle with basic drafting the way we used to struggle. But again, your voice isn't a tool you find and *then* start using; **your *voice* is just another term for the confidence you need to say what you really mean to say, the way you really need to say it.**

Writing never becomes *easy*, but eventually it seems less like squeezing yourself through a tube and more like an honest chore, the kind that gives you a real reward for real time and effort. Hardly much cause for complaint by then.

Here are a few tips for finding your own voice, or . . . well, you know what I mean.

Don't feel that you need to be 100% unique to matter. There is nothing new under the sun. If you made something that were *completely* and *truly* original, it would most likely be lunacy. Our very names are recycled, y'all—I bet every person reading this has at least one person on Earth with the same name. My point is that you should not, as a writer, fall under the illusion that you must "write differently" to have value. There are only so many ways to write good English sentences. It's the content of your sentences, and your confidence with that content—not the whimsy of each sentence's construction—that will set your work apart.

To that end, *focus on the fundamentals*. Write things as simply and accurately as you can. Be as clear and concise as you can naturally manage. Pick the neatest words. If something can't be put simply or quickly, it won't have an emotional impact—and if you can't have an emotional impact, you won't be remembered. Consider that some of the loftiest passages in English (like Lincoln's speeches) are composed from a plurality of short, single-syllable words.

When you're at a crucial moment and you don't know how to put something gracefully, *just spit it out*. It might take courage to do that, but it's far more honest than what most people do—which is swallow the truth and write something bland and palatable instead. Remember, you can always edit later.

Be in practice making your writing part of a verbal process (and vice versa). Read your work aloud as you write it; the point is not to "awaken the editor" to scrutinize every word of the chapter, but rather, to "test" certain phrases and see if they roll off your tongue with confidence. For the same reasons, read the work of others—whether fiction or the latest editorials—aloud and see if you notice their "power phrases," or sections where the phrasing and word choice are especially sharp. Lastly, use your own literal voice to get yourself out of writing ruts; if you're unsure what to write, talk it out and see if you can't use one of your own "loose ends."

➔ ACTIVITY ➔

Do a timed writing describing your voice.

PART 5

Before You Publish

You've finished your first draft; now what's next? This section discusses how to work with editors (with an editor serving as guest blogger), how and why to create your own editorial board, and then more about writing those other sections that your book will need—like About the Author, Letter to the Reader, and your book's summary.

WORKING WITH EDITORS
GUEST BLOG FROM BARBARA MCNICHOL

You have a voice, a desire, a dream for your book. It's more than words on paper; it's you. It's your contribution to the world. It needs to come through loud and clear. But how do you make sure that happens?

Big-Picture Blueprint Questionnaire

Let me outline a process that has worked well for me over 23 years and the dozens of authors whose books I've edited. At our first contact, I ask them to complete what I call a Big-Picture Blueprint for Planning Your Nonfiction Book. The objective? Working with this questionnaire gets authors to think about the big-picture aspects of what their book can do for them, their business, their audience, and the world at large.

Initial questions ask to define the Target Audience and Niche or Category. Then they zero in on other goals in areas many authors don't often think about. Here are five key questions:

1. **How would you rank your long-term goals for your book?** Options might be:

   - Become a local or national bestseller in your category
   - Serve as a high-class business card
   - Build your reputation and credibility in your marketplace
   - Provide a product profit center in your business
   - Help you launch a new business

This question is akin to Stephen Covey's habit of starting with the end in mind. It provides a guiding light when the going gets tough. It serves as a guiding light for me when I'm editing the manuscript, too.

2. After people in your target audience have read this book, what do you want them to say about it? Here's where future desired testimonial language would come in. Use your imagination. What would they say? Some version of "Your book is the greatest because ___!" Write something compelling that's specific to your book and powerfully indicates the benefit of your message.

3. What actions do you want people to take as a result of reading your book—both for their own benefit and for yours? For example, if you're writing a leadership book, you might state you want your readers to follow your formula to improve as a leader. That benefits them. But what benefits you? You might jot down they'd buy your book or hire your services or whatever you're aiming to achieve.

4. How will you know when you've met your goals? What measures will you use? For example, you might write "in two years I will have sold 10,000 books" or "I'll have 5,000 new subscribers to my newsletter" or "I've attracted two dozen new clients to my business." Beyond your wildest dreams, what would you want to happen?

5. What intrinsic value would having a successful book bring to your business? It might be the same as the measurable goals stated above, but more likely it has to do with reputation-building or becoming a thought leader in your area of expertise.

Take a few minutes to answer questions 1–5 for yourself right now. Your answers could pertain to a book you've already written or one that's in the planning stage or one that's half-baked. Then find another author or two, share your answers, and ask for suggestions to stretch your thinking.

Two additional Blueprint questions refer to the editing process itself.

6. What dollar amount will you invest in editing to realize the value you want to receive from your book? This gets into expectations around fees and determines if you're on the same page with the editor. If your expectations of a fee is far apart from the editor's standard fee, it signals a discussion is needed.

7. Which results do you seek most in working with an editor? Check all that apply. A list of possibilities gets at the results you want your editor to deliver. Authors most commonly state they look to editors who will help in ways such as . . .

    - eliminate jargon, wordiness, and redundancies
    - embed suggestions for additional content and clarification
    - preserve their voice—a big concern

--➤

Preserving your voice is especially crucial when working with an editor. #Blog2Book

◀--

Preserving your voice is especially crucial, I agree. After all, it's your ideas and solutions going out into the world. You want your readers to "get" who you are and what you do. The best compliment I can ever receive after the editing is, "You made my writing sound like me only better."

Preserving Your Voice through the Magic of a Sample Edit

So how will you know if your voice will be preserved?

Well, here's where the magic lies both for you, the author, and for me, the editor. It's in the Sample Edit, which has been an essential part of my process over the years.

I do a three- or four-page complimentary Sample Edit of YOUR work from YOUR manuscript. Sure, you might get value from seeing the Before and After of someone else's book, but you and I can get on the same page reviewing a Sample Edit from your own work. In fact, if you're interviewing several editors, be sure to ask each one for a Sample Edit. That's how to come closer to comparing apples to apples when you review their work.

So what is the magic in the Sample Edit? Three things:

1. You see exactly how the editor approaches what you've written.
2. You see for yourself if the edits changed your voice.
3. You and I share common ground for discussing the level of editing required.

Then after the Sample Edit, one or two things happen. I either deem your manuscript is ready for nitty-gritty Content/Copy editing or I recommend a Manuscript Review.

Manuscript Review Option

What's a Manuscript Review? It's a macro edit that's often called *developmental editing*. Here's how it works in my world. I read your manuscript and analyze its outline and content. I assess how well the chapters you've written meet the goals stated in your Blueprint. Then I provide written suggestions on how to make specific structural and strategic changes, or make the changes directly.

The Manuscript Review ensures your writing actually aligns with what you intended to write. And in the long run, it ensures the nitty-gritty Content/Copy Editing goes more smoothly, takes less time, and costs less money.

Content/Copy Editing Option

Your manuscript is deemed ready for the complete Content/Copy Editing if you can answer "yes" to these three questions:

- Have you finalized the number and sequencing of your chapters?
- Have you re-evaluated all content yourself and even had peers review it?
- The most important question: Does the manuscript include all the content you want?

Suppose you've answered a triple "yes" and accepted my Editing Plan. Whoopee! From there, you can typically expect three reviews of your manuscript:

1. An initial edit with corrections, questions, suggestions—equivalent to a full massage, not a fluff-and-buff approach to your writing.
2. A second review incorporates all of the changes/additions you make after you work through the first review suggestions.
3. A final proofread is done to catch lingering language and format glitches.

This outline makes the process sound simple, right? Editors do their best to streamline the process for all involved. Yet the human factor always comes into play, so make sure you choose an editor who has your best interests in mind superseding strict rules and processes.

Mostly, you want to select an editor who cares about making your contribution to the world come through loud and clear—in your voice.

___

➔ ACTIVITY ⬅

Answer Barbara's questions outlined above.

___

THE EDITORIAL BOARD

No matter how careful you are, you are not going to catch everything on your own. No editor is perfect, but you are *especially* not a perfect editor since you are also the author in this case. Get another person to look it over; if you can get more than one person to examine things, that's even better. If those different editors are better at helping with different things, that's better yet. Pull in as many sets of cold eyes as you can, and you'll get as close to the "perfect version" of your book as you can.

To be specific, see if you can't consult the help of:

- Authors
- Professionals in your field
- Clients and prospective clients
- Fellow thought leaders or other people you respect professionally
- Industry leaders and senior executives
- Professional editors

To the best of your ability, provide them with specific direction for editing, and ask them specific questions of the work they return to you. You might have a given person focus on just one thing, or you might have them look at several items, but you should be purposeful in your direction in either case.

- ▶

No editor is perfect, but you are especially
not a perfect editor since you are also
the author in this case. #Blog2Book

◀ -

For example, I asked Lisa Braithwaite, a client working on her own Blog2Book book, to review this as someone who is putting together her own. I also asked Mark Coile, who is beginning his blog this month, to review it from the standpoint of a new blogger. I asked another friend, Elizabeth Jeffries, to see if the book flowed well, and I also asked her about the book title (I had a different subtitle early on and it didn't seem to fit me).

If you are writing about Human Resources issues, you might ask a Human Resources practitioner to review with practitioners in mind. You might ask an academic to review it to ensure it has the proper grounding and research. In other words, focus on the ways in which your editorial board can best examine the book from many perspectives and provide feedback based upon their experience and expertise.

You may want your editorial board to provide their expertise by answering your own set of specific questions, such as:

- Have I answered my readers' questions?
- Does the book flow? Does it make sense?
- Is the book clear? If not, what needs clarification or illustration?
- Is the book practical? If not, what could be added?
- What seems contradictory?

And, especially for Blog2Book books, you may ask your editorial board:

- Is the subject matter fully covered?What is redundant?
- Does the book have a unified voice?
- Does the book need introductions for each of its parts?
- Are all of the chapters evergreen?

⊙ ACTIVITY ⊙

Create your ideal editorial board. Schedule a conversation with them,
and see if they are on board. Let them know what you want of them,
and the time period that your manuscript will be ready for their review.

  **BLOG POST**

CHECKLIST FOR YOUR BOOK

You're almost done with your book—or are you? Do you have all the pieces you'll need to begin work with your publisher?

Here is a checklist of the components of your book you'll need to gather so that you'll be ready to move forward with your publisher.

Cover

- Title and subtitle
- Cover art (if you have any in mind)
- Book summary for back of book
- Testimonials (1 to 3 of the best quotes)
- Author photo (recent, high-resolution)

-->

You're almost done with your book—or are you? #Blog2Book

<---

Front Matter

- Table of Contents
- Letter to the Reader
- Introduction
- How to Use This Book
- Foreword
- Acknowledgements
- About the Author
- Dedication

Contents

- All body content
- Permissions, as needed
- Call-outs or pull quotes (consider "tweetable" selections)
- External quotes
- Graphics or photos to be included
- Sidebars, insets, other boxed/side text

Back Matter

- Contact information and website links
- Index
- Glossary
- Appendices
- Resources (I suggest putting these on your website if you have one)

⊙ ACTIVITY ⊙

Use this checklist to determine what pieces, if any, are missing.
Create a schedule to complete these pieces.

ABOUT THE AUTHOR

You're going to use your "About the Author" information in many places. You'll use an abbreviated version on your book jacket or cover, and you'll likely have a longer version within the book. You'll include a bio on your one-sheet for promoting your book and speaking; you'll include a bio on your website; you'll need an introduction for speaking, and for book readings and signings.

How much do you write, and what should your "About the Author" include?

---------------------------------------→

You're going to use your "About the Author" information in many places. #Blog2Book

←---------------------------------------

To create your bio, I recommend you start with a series of short writing exercises. Put five or ten minutes on your timer, and then conduct these four writing sprints (no thinking and no editing, just writing). You can make a list or merely jot down words or phrases. Don't try to write a narrative.

Outline your greatest accomplishments and credentials related to the book's topic. What is the highest position you've held? What is the most prestigious organization you've led? What is your highest educational attainment? What awards or recognition have you earned for your work?

Describe the work you do for clients. Tell more about how you provide value for your clients. Why do your clients call on you? How do you help your clients in ways others don't or can't? What are the problems you solve?

What are your highest-held beliefs and values? How do they relate to this book? How does the book speak to your personal mission, to what's most important to you?

What are some fun facts about you? Do you have hobbies or interests related to your topic—or completely unrelated to your topic? Have you been to exotic places? Have you done something outrageous?

You should now have four lists. For a short bio, take one sentence from each. For a medium-length bio, take two sentences from each list. For a longer bio, take three or more sentences from each. Voila—your bio has been drafted!

Here's one way to have someone introduce you, as suggested by National Speakers Association member Christine Cashen: first, start with three questions to which your audience can answer "yes."

"Do you have a book inside you but don't know how to get it out?
"Do you know the value of a book and how it can be a powerful business development tool?
"Do you want an easy-to-follow process that will take you from blog to book?"

Now, present a few of the credentials and describe the work you do. (Don't overdo it, or make anyone roll their eyes; just make yourself sound credible.)

"Our speaker today is the author of eight books . . ."

Then, add something fun. "You may not know that our speaker today . . . "

Conclude the introduction with some fanfare: "And now, please welcome our speaker from Louisville, Kentucky, the Business Book Strategist, Cathy Fyock!"

⊙ ACTIVITY ⊙

Do the writing exercises, then create a short, medium, and long "About the Author." Lastly, write an introduction for yourself. Print the introduction, put it in a sheet protector, and take it to all your speaking and book-launch events.

LETTER TO YOUR READER

In my work as a book coach, I've found that the single most helpful writing prompt is this: "Write a letter to your reader."

This writing prompt is powerful because it keeps you focused on the person you're trying to help, and in the ways you're trying to help them. After all: while your book may be about you and your ideas, it is *for* your readers, and no author should ever forget that.

I especially love the letter to your reader as an exercise because it can be repurposed as an introduction for your book. (And you know what I think about repurposing!)

- ⟶

Write a letter to your reader. #Blog2Book

⟵ -

Another exercise is creating a list of your readers' characteristics. Are they young or old on average? Men or women? Professionals or non-professionals? The more specific you can be in your descriptions, the better you'll be able to speak to your readers' needs and concerns.

An alternate exercise is to write a story about your reader. Put five or ten minutes on the clock. Go.

These exercises force you to make a habit of examining your book from your readers' perspective. It forces you to define your reader in specific and meaningful ways, and it allows you to see your work through your readers' eyes.

Some authors find that a picture representing their reader—perhaps some kind of photograph or illustration—is useful when printed out and posted near their desk or writing space. Some authors might think about a specific client or colleague and hold them in mind while writing their books.

The "letter to my reader" writing prompt is one that can (and should) be revisited throughout the writing of the blog or book. It consistently returns the author to their readers' perspective, which is the one most important for the book to honor. Subsequent prompts may also unearth new insights or perspectives that can prove helpful when fine-tuning the book's approach.

⮕ ACTIVITY ⬅

Write a letter to your reader. Write a story about your reader.
Create a list of target reader characteristics.
Find a picture that represents your reader, then print it and post it.

WRITING YOUR BOOK SUMMARY

You'll need a book summary for the back cover of your book and for reader descriptions online, on venues such as Amazon and other booksellers' websites (including your own). Your book summary will appear on your one-sheet, on social media pages, and virtually everywhere your book is mentioned (think *media releases*).

For those who wrote a book proposal to submit to an agent or publisher, this is your compelling "sizzle paragraph" which highlights not just what the book is about, but why *this book*, why *now*, and why written by *you*.

--→

Your book summary will appear on your one-sheet, on social media pages, and virtually everywhere your book is mentioned. #Blog2Book

←--

This short paragraph is probably the most important paragraph you will write for your book, since it will be the paragraph that compels a reader to pick up, buy, and read your book.

Book summaries may include statistics, quotes, or short anecdotes that connect with your reader. The summary might also discuss why readers need this book, how this book solves a problem that plagues the target reading audience.

The summary should begin with a strong opening sentence. (See Chapter 23 for information about creating compelling openings for blog posts).

Here is the summary paragraph for *On Your Mark*:

You have a book inside you, but how do you get it out? Author Cathy Fyock has written five of her six books in less than six weeks, and has a formula for getting the book out of your head and heart and onto the written page. She and coauthor Kevin Williamson offer tips for identifying your obstacles, turning off "that voice" inside your head, getting a game plan, creating momentum, and finishing your draft. With their practical tips and exercises, you'll finish with an action plan for getting your book done!

Some questions your summary paragraph should answer:

- Have you answered the question *What is this book about?*
- Have you provided a call to action?
- Have you identified the value to the reader?

➡ ACTIVITY ⬅

*Write a short (75-100 words) and a long (150-250 words)
book summary for your book.*

PART 6

Publishing and Promoting

Many published authors agree that the writing of the book is just a small part of the total equation. Another time-consuming and vital component for your book is the publishing and promoting of your book. This section outlines ideas for getting endorsements (those great blurbs that appear on your book's cover, inside the book, and perhaps as reviews on Amazon), for considering self-publishing, and for launching your blog book.

✹ NEW POST

ENDORSEMENTS

Once you've written the book draft and are preparing to send the book to your editorial board, you might begin collecting testimonials—or blurbs—about your book at the same time.

These are the pieces of written social proof that tell the world how fabulous your book is, what a wonderful speaker or consultant or coach you are, and why your target reader should run out and buy this book right away.

You might use testimonials on the book cover (one to three of the best), in the front matter just inside the book, on your website, or on your book's one-sheet and other marketing materials. You can't have enough of these—and there are tons of places you can use them to buff yourself up!

-->

Use testimonials on the book cover, in the front matter, on your website, or on your book's one-sheet and marketing materials. #Blog2Book

<--

First: create a list of your friends, colleagues, clients, and others who are on your support team and assemble their contact information. Who do you know that is a "name" in your industry or with your target reader? Next, think about your "wish list" for book testimonials. Whose testimonials would you and your readers value? What thought leaders and industry leaders would lend credibility to your book if their name were attached to a testimonial?

When I wrote my third book, *UnRetirement*, I was thinking about who was then (in the mid-nineties) a "name" in the aging workforce arena. I immediately thought of Art Linkletter, who had written his book *Old Age Is Not For Sissies* in 1988. I also knew that Art was a fellow member of the National Speakers Association—and I thought, *why not see if Art would be willing to endorse my book? What's the worst that could happen?*

Long story short, Art was delighted to endorse my book, and he provided a glowing testimonial that I used on the book cover and in all of the promotional literature.

The moral of the story: don't be shy about asking for an endorsement, even if it's the biggest name you can think of.

Once you've created your wish list and found contact information, you will either want to call or email each person on your list to request their support.

Below is the email template I used when writing to generate support for *On Your Mark* . . .

I'm authoring an exciting new book, and I'm writing you to see if you would be willing to write an endorsement and join my support team!

My book, co-authored with my nephew, Kevin Williamson, is titled, On Your Mark: From First Word to First Draft in Six Weeks. *The intended audience are those who dream of writing a book, especially those who want or need a book as a tool for business development. Speakers, consultants, coaches, business leaders, bloggers, and academicians are part of my audience.*

If you are interested and willing, I can send you either a sample chapter or the entire book (approximately 30,000+ words). I am able to send you the sample chapter now, and if you'd like the entire book, I will be able to send it to you in the next couple of weeks (as Kevin finishes his sections).

I need a short, punchy endorsement from you that I plan to use on the book jacket and in marketing and publicity for the book. I'll need this as soon as possible since I'll begin working with my publisher shortly. Please be sure to indicate how you would like your name/title to appear.

If, in addition to writing an endorsement, you might be willing to give me a shout-out on your web site, on blog posts, or in your social media, I'd love to work with you. Let me know what would be most helpful in us working together.

I'm beginning my new business in January, focusing on helping those who dream of writing their book get it done in 6 weeks. I'll offer group coaching and one-on-one coaching in addition to my book; I'd appreciate any referrals you might have. I also hope to speak on this topic (and in writing articles and blogs to build one's business), so if you know of groups who would like to hear my message, please let me know.

My new email address is cathy@cathyfyock.com, and my telephone remains 502-445-6539.

Let me know if you'd like to chat about my new venture; I'm looking forward to hearing from you. Thanks so much for your continued friendship and support!

— Cathy

In addition to sending this first email, I followed up with many people afterwards by phone or with a second email.

➔ ACTIVITY ➔

Create a list of those you'll invite to endorse your book.
Don't forget friends, colleagues, clients, prospects, authors, speakers, and other thought leaders in your industry.
Also, consider the biggest name that would add credibility and/or visibility to your book, and invite that individual.

51

SELF-PUBLISHING:
"I'M BUILDING A HOME"

What does it mean when your friends say that they're building a house? Does it mean that they're drafting the floor plans, trucking in the lumber, and putting up framing and drywall? Does it mean that they're building the frame and getting a plumber and electrician to finish it? Or, more likely, does it mean that they have *paid for* the building of a house—that they hired a contractor (and company) to get it built with skilled hands, according to your specs?

The truth of the matter is that all three scenarios are "building a home." Building a home can be a complete DIY on one end of the spectrum, or on the other end, hiring someone to do all the aspects of building for you and never lifting a hammer yourself.

Similarly, self-publishing your book offers the same range of options. On one end of the spectrum, you can edit your book yourself (totally not advisable), design your own book cover, and publish the book by your own means. In the middle, you can hire professionals to do certain tasks for you. At the other end of the spectrum, you can hire a self-publishing company to manage all the steps.

What should you be looking for in a self-publishing company? Typically, a self-publishing firm can provide you with the following range of services:

1. Developmental editing
2. Copy editing
3. Formatting, both for e-book and for POD (print on demand)
4. Library of Congress (LOC) number
5. ISBN

6. Cover design
7. Placement on Amazon
8. Website development
9. Marketing support

As you explore these different options, determine the following:

- How much time do I want to spend becoming an expert in publishing?
- What is my budget?
- What are my strengths and weaknesses?
- What are my technical skillsets?
- How much time can I spend on this project?
- What is my deadline for completing the project?

Additional questions to ask:

- What are the values that my publishing company espouses?
- What niche market does the publishing company serve?
- How does their value weigh against their costs?
- Who do I trust? Who do I want to work with?

Like building a home, picking a publishing partner requires trust and mutual respect. Be sure you do your homework to ensure you are selecting the right partner to meet your publishing goals.

⊙ ACTIVITY ⊙

Review the questions, then begin exploring different publishing options.
Schedule interviews with at least 2 publishing companies to learn more about
the field and, if possible, determine the best fit for your needs.

LAUNCHING YOUR BLOG BOOK

Maybe you've just started on your book. Maybe you're almost done. Wherever you are in the process, it's not too late to begin to promote your book NOW.

Here are twenty simple things you can do before your book is launched. Begin your action planning NOW!

1. Get the cover art completed for the book. This is a big visual asset, so begin using it; consider adding the picture to your email signature and website.

2. Ask ten or more influential friends, colleagues, clients, or readers to review all or part of the book and provide you with short, punchy testimonials that you can use to promote the book. Include these in the front section of your book, on the book's cover, and on other promotional materials.

3. Create or update your website; include the picture of the book's cover, a short description of the book, and a compelling testimonial (collected in #2). Pre-sell the book or push for readers to buy on your launch date.

4. Add "Author of the forthcoming book" to your email signature (along with the cover art, as you added in #1).

5. Create a media list which might include your local paper, alumni publications, and membership organizations with available contact information. Develop a list of other interest groups that would want to know about your book (for example, various Human Resources organizations if your book is for HR professionals).

6. Create a one-sheet describing the book.

7. Create a postcard or bookmark—some small printing that represents the book. Include the book's cover, a short description, and

a testimonial. When you need more business cards, consider adding your book's cover to the back of your card.

8. Write media releases to send to the list you generated in #5.
9. Write an article on the topic of your book drawing a connection to current news—or just excerpt articles from the book. Wherever you have publication opportunities, indicate the connection to your forthcoming book—ideally with information on how to find and order it.
10. Set dates for book launch parties. Realize that your family, friends, colleagues, and readers want to be a part of these exciting, celebratory events whenever they can. And don't forget that you can schedule "live" parties as well as "virtual" parties (delivered via webinar for out-of-town contacts).
11. Create a list to invite to your book launch parties (virtual and live). Build your database now and always to expand your platform.
12. Begin promoting your book on social media with teasers about your book's topic. Be sure to use pictures of your book cover when possible. Start a Facebook page for your book. Promote your book launch parties via Facebook events and other social media outlets.
13. Pre-sell books on your website.
14. Create a signature for autographing your book. For example, when I sign copies of my book *On Your Mark: From First Word to First Draft in Six Weeks*, I sign, "Make your mark!"

- ->

Tell everyone about your new book. #Blog2Book

<- -

15. Create a presentation on your book's topic. It can be for webinars, keynotes, workshops, or facilitations and readings for book club meetings.
16. Build your database of direct contacts, including those on social media.
17. Create a one-page flyer on your speaking topics related to the book. Include your speaking credentials and testimonials about you as a speaker.
18. Develop "tweetable" clips from the book to use to promote your book on Twitter—remember, they're 140 characters or less. Create your

own hashtag for your book (for example, my last book's hashtag is #HallelujahTheBook).

19. Wear a magic button that says *Ask Me About My Book* when you attend networking events or travel on business. (I give these to my coaching clients, and I always wear mine!)

20. Tell *everyone* about your new book. It creates excitement and energy about the book's release if you're excited about it and want to share!

❯ ACTIVITY ❮

Review the list and determine which items you can begin now.
Create a calendar for the activities you'll schedule now
through six months to one year post-publication.

FINAL THOUGHTS
WHY WOULD ANYBODY WANT TO READ MY STORY?

Why would anybody want to read my story?

It was an innocent question a client asked me during a strategy session. Ever since I've begun full-time work with books and publishing, it's a question that I've heard repeatedly from aspiring authors.

I've thought a great deal about how to answer that question. I've discovered that one's answer to that question is rooted in belief—and so my answer is given as a series of beliefs about the purpose of our lives and the role books and stories play in that purpose.

I hope that, by sharing these beliefs with you, I might help inspire you to discover your own purpose through writing—and to share your story with others.

I believe that we are created with a purpose.

I believe that we each have value and significance.

I believe that we all have unique experiences that shape our lives and provide us with a perspective not shared by anyone else.

I believe that we can help others by sharing our stories, our experiences, what we've learned along the way.

I believe that when we tell our stories, we allow others to bear witness to the purpose of our lives.

I believe that everyone can help someone by sharing their story, especially stories of how we've dealt with adversity.

I believe that our stories give others the gifts of hope, wisdom, encouragement, laughter, insight, joy.

---➤

I believe that is it holy work in writing and telling your story, and it is also holy work in helping people tell their stories. #Blog2Book

◄---

I believe that you can never know the full impact of your story on others.

I believe that if you impact just one person in a positive way by telling your story, that impact gives meaning and purpose to your life.

I believe that books are the documents that contain our stories, and therefore, help to document our purpose.

I believe that is it holy work in writing and telling your story, and it is also holy work in helping people tell their stories.

What is your purpose? What does writing your story mean to you? What do you believe? I welcome your comments and thoughts about the power of sharing your story as testament to your purpose.

ACKNOWLEDGEMENTS

Many thanks to my clients and colleagues who gave me the idea for this book. I'd like to extend special thanks to Lois Creamer and Lisa Braithwaite, who became my first Blog2Book clients.

A full round of applause for my fabulous editorial board: Elizabeth Jeffries, Whitney Martin, Lisa Braithwaite, and Mark Coile. I so appreciate each of your efforts.

I could not have written this book without support from my editor, publisher, and nephew Kevin Williamson. Many thanks to Kevin for his continued love, support, and brilliant writing.

I'd also like to thank my MasterMind groups for their support, and my clients for continuing to give me good ideas about how to best serve writers who want to tell their stories.

RESOURCES

For more information about resources and coaching services, visit Cathy's website:

www.CathyFyock.com

or call Cathy directly at **502.445.6539**.

ABOUT THE AUTHOR

Cathy Fyock, CSP, SPHR, SHRM-SCP is the Business Book Strategist. Cathy works with thought leaders and professionals who want to write a book as a business development strategy.

Cathy is the author of seven other books:

- *America's Work Force is Coming of Age*
- *Get The Best*
- *UnRetirement*
- *Hiring Source Book*
- *The Truth About Hiring The Best*
- *On Your Mark: From First Word to First Draft in Six Weeks*
- *Hallelujah! An Anthem for Purposeful Work*

In addition to her work helping her clients become published, she has served as project lead for five professional anthologies: *What's Next in Human Resources, Rethinking Human Resources, Lessons in Leadership, Evolution of Human Resources,* and *Cultivating Culture.*

Cathy believes whole-heartedly that we are each created with purpose, that by telling and writing our stories we allow others to bear witness to the purpose of our lives. She believes it is holy work to write and tell your stories.

Cathy is a lifelong singer and longtime member of her church choir. She resides in Louisville, Kentucky with Jim, her husband of more than 40 years.

Cathy can be reached by email at cathy@cathyfyock.com or by phone at 502.445.6539.

CPSIA information can be obtained
at www.ICGtesting.com
Printed in the USA
FSOW04n0614120117
29349FS